THE
ETHICS
OF
SPINOZA

THE
ETHICS
OF
SPINOZA

THE ROAD TO INNER FREEDOM

Edited by Dagobert D. Runes

A Citadel Press Book
Published by Carol Publishing Group

First Carol Publishing Group Edition 1991

A Citadel Press Book
Published by Carol Publishing Group

Editorial Offices
600 Madison Avenue
New York, NY 10022

Sales & Distribution Offices
120 Enterprise Avenue
Secaucus, NJ 07094

In Canada: Musson Book Company
A division of General Publishing Co. Limited
Don Mills, Ontario

Citadel Press is a registered trademark of
Carol Communications, Inc.

Manufactured in the United States of America
ISBN 0-8065-0787-X

12 11 10 9 8 7 6 5 4

Carol Publishing Group books are available at special discounts
for bulk purchases, for sales promotions, fund raising, or
educational purposes. Special editions can also be created to
specifications. For details contact: Special Sales Department,
Carol Publishing Group, 120 Enterprise Ave., Secaucus, NJ 07094

The text is based on the translation by
R.H.M. Elwes. Changes and revisions were
made by the editor after reference to
the Bruder Latin edition of the text.

CONTENTS

A Word to the Reader

A Word
to the Reader

In 1492, the year of the discovery of America, the shadow of religious persecution fell across the Iberian peninsula. The Jews of Spain were set upon by church and state, and under the threat of dire consequences, were expelled to the four corners of the world.

Among those who fled for their lives, first to Portugal and then to the haven of Holland, were the ancestors of Baruch Spinoza. Spinoza's father, Michael, settled in Amsterdam, and it is there our philosopher spent his youth. The elder Spinoza was a thrice married man, and from all indications, his household lived in constant turmoil.

Spinoza experienced the savagery of religious strife as well as the torment of emotional insecurity. Thus we can readily understand his never-ceasing efforts to free himself and his fellowman from both.

The life and work of this ailing Portuguese Jew of post-Renaissance Holland were dedicated to the search for a way to human happiness and social dignity.

How to bring about peace of faith and peace of mind were both the early and the mature goals of Spinoza.

He was sickened by the complicated theological disputations that could result in danger to life and limb because of refusal to accept a comma or a word. Scholastic as well as talmudic argumentation, like the constantly dangling sword of the Inquisition—Catholic as well as Protestant—drove him to cry out against religion as a system of knowledge.

The Bible is God's word to the people, he exclaimed, and not to the priests and preachers. Faith is a matter of love, not of knowledge, and to worship means to live in justice and charity. To do good is the only true law of the Torah, and those who are zealots of the letter of the law are not God's defenders, but His enemies.

These concepts are evident even in the young Spinoza, identifying the Hebrew mitzvah, or commandment, with mitzvah in its other meaning of Godbinding.

This stress on the spirit of Judaism, rather than its legalism, was the earliest expression of a new ideology which in later centuries became the basis of the Jewish Reform movement.

I do not know of any modern philosopher of note more intimately tied to the basic concepts of Judaism than is Spinoza. His melancholy observations on the vanities of life and vacillating mankind are deeply stamped by the cogitations of Ecclesiastes.

He profoundly expounded the love of intuitive wisdom which accompanies man's awareness of God as the all pervading eternity, the *Echod* and *Ain Soph*, the One and the Infinite, that can and will conquer the little pleasures of irrational selfishness. He defended heroically and insistently the Hebraic principles of justice and the rights of man in a free community subservient to no entity but the law of the Lord. One can say that through every thought and word of the philosopher Spinoza there breathes the *Ruach Hakodesh*, the Spirit of Holiness of Judaism. Spinoza may rightly be called *Judaissimus*, the most Jewish of all thinkers.

With Spinoza, Judaism took its first steps away from the system of orthodox observance. And from the day when Spinoza's first work appeared, no one could ever write of Jewish problems without taking issue with the Sage of Rijnsburg.

Spinoza's passionate attitude toward religion as a thing of life rather than of doctrine, when carried over into his political philosophy, culminated in the proposition that the business of the state is security for its citizens and nothing else. Therefore, freedom of thought and freedom of speech are the fundamental rights of the citizen.

In his books as well as in his letters, Spinoza pleaded for political and religious freedom, for the right of man to speak freely on whatever moved his mind. Seventeenth century Europe was torn by religious strife, and it was only natural for the issue of man's civil rights to become paramount in his thought.

Spinoza was the philosopher with a purpose *par excellence*.

The fundamentals of philosophy in all its aspects served him only as the base upon which to erect his principles of the ideal free man.

The free man, viewing the world before him as part of the infinite universe, was for Spinoza the scope and purpose of all cogitation.

To live as the master of one's emotions and passions, that was in the final analysis the goal of Spinoza's study in Ethics. How to reach that goal, to see the panorama of daily existence *sub specie aeternitatis,* he endeavored to explain in the book before us.

While these lofty ideals are ever appealing to us, we must, on the other hand, try to understand that Spinoza's co-religionists, leaning upon each other for succor and support, were terrified at Spinoza's disavowal of the 613 precepts of the Torah, which he maintained were state regulations of Israel and valid only for that state, which no longer existed. The orthodox Jews of Amsterdam were concerned to the utmost lest the young man's reduction of the Torah from a book of law, history and ritual to a mere volume of theistic inspiration would lead other men out of the fold of the Hebrew community.

This anxiety, and no other reason, caused the synagogal authorities to try to stop the proselytizing rebel, and when all other means failed, they finally placed upon him the heavy shroud of excommunication.

＊　　＊

Spinoza spoke ahead of his time and ahead of his people. It took more than a hundred years for mankind to fall into step with his thinking, and it took more than three hundred years for the People of the Book to realize that they had to return to their prodigal son.

Ruach Hakodesh pervades the writings of Baruch Spinoza, the Holy Spirit that has breathed through the wisdom literature of Israel from the days of the philosopher king, Solomon, and even earlier.

Spinoza's *amor Dei intellectualis,* the spiritual love of God, is closest to the Hebrew *simchah shel mitzvah,* the joy of faith, the joy of the law. In the ideology of Spinoza, living by the law of wisdom was identical with obedience to the divine principle.

The teachings of the Cabala had a tremendous influence upon him. The cardinal idea of the Cabala, the *Ain Soph* (no end-infinite) from which all being emanates, can easily be identified with Spinoza's *Substantia,* the Endless, the All.

＊　　＊

Spinoza's epistemology is based on the three forms of knowledge:

1) vague understanding; 2) reason, and 3) intuition. It bears close resemblance to the Cabalistic

idea of 1) *chochmah,* wisdom; 2) *binah,* reason, and 3) *da at,* perception.

It is obvious that Spinoza would have attempted to hide the Hebrew root of his basic philosophy; his people did not want him, and it was precisely because of differences over interpretation of the teachings of Judaism that he broke with them. He dropped even his name, Baruch, for the Latin Benedictus.

However, looking back over the sobering distance of three hundred years, we must say with all emphasis that the writings of Spinoza are purely and thoroughly Hebraic—root, stem, and fruit.

In the other phases of his writings, those devoted to a better and ethical inner life, Baruch Spinoza also drew his strength from the treasures of the Cabala. The traditional works of Torah, Talmud, and Cabala were a source of enrichment for the young and striving scholar; however, he always managed to brush aside the merely dogmatic in favor of the essential. His heart was set on the core of the script. Forever in search of the *Or Adonai,* the Light of the Lord, he paralleled, in a way, the religious experiences of all great mystics from Lao Tse to Fox, from Buddha to Baal Shem Tov.

For Spinoza, moralizing rules and theological ritual were anything but the true road to ethics.

❖   ❖

Only a great emotion can master the confusing affectations and affections that lie at the root of the evil deeds man commits agains his fellowman; and that great emotion is born out of the love and understanding of God, not as an anthropomorphic tyrant of the heavens, but rather as Creative Nature that in its cosmic infinity is accessible to man's mind through intellectual devotion to reason, justice, and charity.

Indeed, for Spinoza, godliness and humanitarianism, love and wisdom, are identical. There is no higher knowledge than the intuitive love for the divine principle and for one's fellowman; and the greatest happiness comes when man's love has for its object the knowledge of God. In this sense, virtue is its own reward, and whoever has felt the beatitude and intellectual satisfaction wrought by this philosophy will readily forego the quasi advantages offered by the three great greeds that crush man's inner freedom—the greed for riches, the greed for public fame, and the greed for the unrestrained satisfaction of lust.

＊　＊

Spinoza begins with a pronounced sense of doubt, accepting little as valid without examination. Traditional concepts of good and evil, pagan and Christian, right and wrong, are cast aside, and fundamental queries are brought up such as: What is God? What is Man? What is Truth? What is Love?

And out of these searching problems rose Spinoza's majestic principles. God is Creative Nature—the Ever-Being, *Ens Perfectissimum*, which we can never think away, and which we can in no way conceive as having been created or as having not existed. The knowledge of God as essence and substance is an inexplicable part of our mind; in fact, it is the essence of our mind. In a mystical sense, our mind is in God; our mind, as the Hebrew sages expressed it, is *Shekinah*, the in-dwelling of God.

To the extent that the human soul envisions God, or Creative Nature, in its one-ness and eternity, the *Elohenu* and *Echod* of Toraic literature become man himself, part of eternity, his ideas clear and adequate and his soul filled with the intellectual love of God, *amor Dei intellectualis*.

This love of God, born out of philosophic insight into the universe in all its formations and modifications, brings a stream of love to fellowman. In fact, the love of man to God is identical with the love of man to man. This *amor Dei intellectualis*, which means no more than awareness of creation in the love of God, or *Adonai*, fills man's soul with a profound sense of gratification and beatitude; and before this great love, man's trifling and disturbing hatreds, prejudices, and other confusing ideas and passions recede into the background.

The disturbing passions are only the bodily manifestations of disturbing ideas: it is the same order or disorder viewed in one instance as a form of the mind and again as a form of the body.

What then is man himself but a mere form or *modus* in God, a mere drop in the ocean of causality, a passing breath in the wind of time?

In the peculiar framework of his existence, man ascribes to God the attributes of space and ideas. Such is the character by which man conceives of Creative Nature; but Creative Nature may be perceived in infinite attributes—space and ideas are only the two formed in man's mind. Endless space and unlimited ideas are man's way in the face of the universe. But the universe, the One and the Ever, is the Infinite *perennis*.

Man can rise from the oblivion of his fleeting existence through the spark of divine cognition. Man himself becomes eternal in contemplating the essence of being. *Shekinah* is the bridge to God; indeed, *God and the intelligence of Him are the same*. The intuitive chain to God is the same as the intuitive chain to man. Man can be a God to man.

Such love born out of the clarity of the mind is the great purifier of the soul, and will bring peace and lasting satisfaction to those who harbor it.

The free man is a seeker of truth, for only true ideas in constant reference to the idea of God can clarify for him the universal concepts that are the basis of his inner happiness. This happiness is not the reward of virtue; this happiness is rather virtue itself and truth itself. Virtue, truth, inner satisfaction, these are identical with the free man's contemplation of God or Creative Nature.

❋ ❋

Baruch Spinoza, expelled by a fearful community of his own faith and damned by the Christian Europe of his era, became the architect of an astonishing philosophical structure that has enriched and enchanted great minds ever since.

From Leibniz to Einstein, from Goethe to Santayana, the near-great and the little people have come to drink from the fountain of life that is Spinoza's *Ethics*.

The steps to this *fons vitae* are many and some are quite steep. I have endeavored to make the path easier for those who may encounter difficulties. It is for the reader to decide whether I have succeeded in the task. I shall be satisfied if I have helped even a few.

D. D. R.

Baruch Spinoza

The Ethics

THE ROAD TO INNER FREEDOM

The Origin and Nature of Emotions

Mathematics
and the Emotional Life

Most writers on the emotions and on human conduct seem to be treating rather of matters outside nature than of natural phenomena following nature's general laws. They appear to conceive man to be situated in nature as a kingdom within a kingdom: for they believe that he disturbs rather than follows nature's order, that he has absolute control over his actions, and that he is determined solely by himself.

They attribute human infirmities and fickleness, not to the power of nature in general, but to some mysterious flaw in the nature of man, which accordingly they bemoan, deride, despise, or, as usually happens, abuse: he, who succeeds in hitting off the weakness of the human mind more eloquently or more acutely than his fellows, is looked upon as a seer.

Still there has been no lack of very excellent men (to whose toil and industry I confess myself much indebted), who have written many noteworthy things concerning the right way of life, and have given much sage advice to mankind. But no one, so far as I know, has defined the nature and strength of the emotions, and the power of the mind against them for their restraint.

I do not forget that the illustrious Descartes, though he believed that the mind has absolute power over its actions, strove to explain human emotions by their primary causes, and, at the same time, to point out a way by which the mind might attain to absolute dominion over them. However, in my opinion, he accomplishes nothing beyond a display of the acuteness of his own great intellect. For the present I wish to revert to those who would rather abuse or deride human emotions than understand them. Such persons will doubtless think it strange that I should attempt to treat of human vice and folly geometrically, and should wish to set forth with rigid reasoning those matters which they cry out against as repugnant to reason, frivolous, absurd, and dreadful. However, such is my plan.

Nothing comes to pass in nature which can be set down to a flaw therein; for nature is always the same, and everywhere one and the same in her efficacy and power of action; that is, *nature's laws and ordinances, whereby all things come to pass and change from one form to another, are everywhere and always the same;* so that there should be one and the same method of understanding the nature of all things whatsoever, namely, through nature's universal laws and rules.

Thus the passions of hatred, anger, envy, and so

on, considered in themselves, follow from this same necessity and efficacy of nature; they answer to certain definite causes, through which they are understood, and possess certain properties as worthy of being known as the properties of anything else, whereof the contemplation in itself affords us delight. I shall, therefore, consider human actions and desires in exactly the same manner as though I were concerned with lines, planes, and solids.

On the Mechanism
of the Human Mind

Our mind is in certain cases active, and in certain cases passive. Insofar as it has adequate ideas it is necessarily active, and insofar as it has inadequate ideas, it is necessarily passive.

Body cannot determine mind to think, neither can mind determine body to motion or rest or any state different from these, if such there be.

This is made more clear by the statement, namely, that mind and body are one and the same thing, conceived first under the attribute of thought, secondly, under the attribute of extension. Thus it follows that the order or concatenation of things is identical, whether nature be conceived under the one attribute or the other; consequently the order of states of activity and passivity in our body is simultaneous in nature with the order of states of activity and passivity in the mind.

Nevertheless, though such is the case, and though there be no further room for doubt, I can scarcely believe, until the fact is proved by experience, that men can be induced to consider the question calmly and fairly, so firmly are they convinced that it is merely at the bidding of the mind that the body is set in motion or at rest, or performs a variety of actions depending solely on the mind's will or the exercise of thought.

However, no one has hitherto laid down the limits to the powers of the body, that is, no one has yet been taught by experience what the body can accomplish solely by the laws of nature, insofar as she is regarded as extension.

No one hitherto has gained such an accurate knowledge of the bodily mechanism, that he can explain all its functions; nor need I call attention to the fact that many actions are observed in the lower animals, which far transcend human sagacity, and that somnambulists do many things in their sleep, which they would not venture to do when awake: these instances are enough to show that the body can by the sole laws of its nature do many things which the mind wonders at.

Again, *no one knows how or by what means the mind moves the body*, nor how many various degrees of motion it can impart to the body, nor how quickly it can move it. Thus, when men say that this or that physical action has its origin in the mind, which latter has dominion over the body, they are using words without meaning, or are confessing in specious phraseology that they are ignorant of the cause of the said action, and do not wonder at it.

But, they will say, whether we know or do not know the means whereby the mind acts on the body, we have, at any rate, experience of the fact that unless the human mind is in a fit state to think, the body remains inert.

Moreover, we have experience that the mind alone can determine whether we speak or are silent, and a variety of similar states which, accordingly, we say depend on the mind's decree. But, as to the first point, I ask such objectors, whether experience does not also teach, that if the body be inactive the mind is simultaneously unfitted for thinking? For when the body is at rest in sleep, the mind simultaneously is in a state of torpor also, and has no power of thinking, such as it possesses when the body is awake.

Again, I think everyone's experience will confirm the statement that the mind is not at all times equally fit for thinking on a given subject, but according as the body is more or less fitted for being stimulated by the image of this or that object, so also is the mind more or less fitted for contemplating the said object.

But, it will be argued, it is impossible that solely from the laws of nature considered as extended substance, we should be able to deduce the causes of buildings, pictures, and things of that kind, which are produced only by human art; nor would the human body, unless it were determined and led by the mind, be capable of building a single temple. However, I have just pointed out that the objectors cannot fix the limits of the body's power, or say what can be concluded from a consideration of its sole nature, whereas they have experience of many things being accomplished solely by the laws of nature, which they would never have believed possible except under the direction of mind: such are the actions performed by somnambulists while asleep, and wondered at by their performers when awake.

I would further call attention to the mechanism of the human body, which far surpasses in complexity all that has been put together by human art, not to repeat what I have already shown, namely, that from nature, under whatever attribute she be considered, infinite results follow.

As for the second objection, I submit that *the world would be much happier, if men were as fully able to keep silence as they are to speak.* Experience abundantly shows that men can govern anything more easily than their tongues, and restrain anything more easily than their appetites; whence it comes about that many believe that we are only free in respect to objects which we moderately desire, because our desire for such can easily be controlled by the thought of something else frequently remembered, but that we are by no means free in respect to what we seek with violent emotion, for our desire cannot then be allayed with the remembrance of anything else.

However, unless such persons had proved by experience that we do many things which we afterwards repent of, and again that we often, when assailed by contrary emotions, see the better and follow the worse, there would be nothing to prevent their believing that we are free in all things. Thus an infant believes that of its own free will it desires milk, an angry child believes that it freely desires vengeance, a timid child believes that it freely desires to run away; further, a drunken man believes that he utters from the free decision of his mind words which, when he is sober, he would willingly have withheld: thus, too, a delirious man, a garrulous woman, a child, and others of like complexion, believe that they speak from the free decision of their mind, when they are in reality unable to restrain their impulse to talk.

Experience teaches us no less clearly than reason, that *men believe themselves to be free, simply because they are conscious of their actions,* and unconscious of the causes whereby those actions are determined; and further, it is plain that the dictates of the mind are but another name for the appetites, and therefore vary according to the varying state of the body.

Everyone shapes his actions according to his emotion. Those who are assailed by conflicting emotions know not what they wish; those who are not attacked by any emotion are readily swayed this way or that. All these considerations clearly show that a mental decision and a bodily appetite, or determined state, are *simultaneous*, or rather are one and the same thing, which we call decision, when it is regarded under and explained through the attribute of thought, and a conditioned state, when it is regarded under the attribute of extension, and deduced from the laws of motion and rest.

For the present I wish to call attention to another point, namely, that we cannot act by the decision of the mind, unless we have a remembrance of having done so. For instance we cannot say a word without remembering that we have done so.

Again, it is not within the free power of the mind to remember or forget a thing at will. Therefore the freedom of the mind must in any case be limited to the power of uttering or not uttering something which it remembers. But when we dream that we speak, we believe that we speak from a free decision of the mind, yet we do not speak, or, if we do, it is by a spontaneous motion of the body. Again, we dream that we are concealing something, and we seem to act from the same decision of the mind as that whereby we keep silence when awake concerning something we know. Lastly, we dream that from the free decision of our mind we do something, which we should not dare to do when awake.

Now I should like to know whether there be in

the mind two sorts of decisions, one sort illusive, and the other sort free? If our folly does not carry us so far as this, we must necessarily admit that the decision of the mind, which is believed to be free, is not distinguishable from the imagination or memory, and is nothing more than the affirmation, which an idea, by virtue of being an idea, necessarily involves. Wheretofore these decisions of the mind arise in the mind by the same necessity, as the ideas of things actually existing. Therefore those who believe that they speak or keep silence or act in any way from the free decision of their mind, do but dream with their eyes open.

The activities of the mind arise solely from adequate ideas; the passive states of the mind depend solely on inadequate ideas.

Nothing can be destroyed, except by a cause external to itself.

Things are naturally contrary, that is, cannot exist in the same object, insofar as one is capable of destroying the other.

Everything, insofar as it is in itself, endeavors to persist in its own being.

The endeavor, wherewith everything endeavors to persist in its own being, is nothing else but the actual essence of the thing in question.

The mind, both insofar as it has clear and distinct ideas, and also insofar as it has confused ideas, endeavors to persist in its being for an indefinite period, and of this endeavor it is conscious. This endeavor, when referred solely to the mind, is called *will*, when referred to the mind and body in conjunction it is called *appetite*; it is, in fact, nothing else but man's essence, from the nature of which necessarily follow all those results which tend to its preservation; and which man has thus been determined to perform.

Further, between appetite and desire there is no difference, except that the term desire is generally applied to men, insofar as they are conscious of their appetite, and may accordingly be thus defined: *Desire is appetite with consciousness thereof.* It is thus plain from what has been said, that in no case do we strive for, wish for, long for, or desire anything because we deem it good, but on the other hand we deem a thing to be good because we strive for it, wish for it, long for it, or desire it.

Whatever increases or diminishes, helps or hinders the power of activity in our body, the idea thereof increases or diminishes, helps or hinders the power of thought in our mind.

Thus we see that the mind can undergo many changes, and can pass sometimes to a state of greater perfection, sometimes to a state of lesser perfection. These passive states of transition explain to us the emotions of pleasure and pain. By *pleasure* therefore in the following propositions I shall signify *a passive state wherein the mind passes to a greater perfection.* By *pain* I shall signify *a passive state wherein the mind passes to a lesser perfection.* Further, the emotion of pleasure in reference to the body and mind together I shall call *stimulation* or *merriment,* the emotion of pain in the same relation I shall call *suffering* or *melancholy.* But we must bear in mind that stimulation and suffering are attributed to man when one part of his nature is more affected than the rest; merriment and melancholy, when all parts are alike affected. What I mean by desire I have explained; beyond these three I recognize no other emotion; I will show as I proceed, that all other emotions arise from these three.

The mind, as far as it can, endeavors to conceive those things which increase or help the power of activity in the body.

When the mind conceives things which diminish or hinder the body's power of activity, it endeavors, as far as possible, to remember things which exclude the existence of the first-named things.

From what has been said we may clearly understand the nature of Love and Hate. *Love* is nothing else but *pleasure accompanied by the idea of an external cause: Hate* is nothing else but *pain accompanied by the idea of an external cause.* We further see, that he who loves necessarily endeavors to have, and to keep present to him, the object of his love; while he who hates endeavors to remove and destroy the object of his hatred.

Anything can, accidentally, be the cause of pleasure, pain, or desire.

Simply from the fact that we have regarded a thing with emotion of pleasure or pain, though that thing be not the efficient cause of the emotion, we can either love or hate it. Hence we understand how it may happen, that we love or hate a thing without any cause for our emotion being known to us; merely, as the phrase is, from *sympathy* or *antipathy*. We should refer to the same category those objects which affect us pleasurably or painfully, simply because they resemble other objects which affect us in the same way.

Simply from the fact that we conceive that a given object has some point of resemblance with another object which is wont to affect the mind pleasurably or painfully, although the point of resemblance be not the efficient cause of the said emotions, we shall still regard the first-named object with love or hate.

If we conceive that a thing, which is wont to affect us painfully, has any point of resemblance with another thing which is wont to affect us with an equally strong emotion of pleasure, we shall hate the first-named thing, and at the same time we shall love it.

If the mind has once been affected by two emotions at the same time, it will, whenever it is afterwards affected by one of the two, be also affected by the other.

This disposition of the mind, which arises from two contrary emotions, is called *vacillation;* it stands to the emotions in the same relation as doubt does to the imagination; vacillation and doubt do not differ one from the other, except as greater differs from less. But we must bear in mind that I have deduced this vacillation from causes, which give rise through themselves to one of the emotions, and to the other accidentally. I have done this, in order that they might be more easily deduced from what went before; but I do not deny that vacillation of the disposition generally arises from an object which is the efficient cause of both emotions. The human body is composed of a variety of individual parts of different nature, and may therefore be affected in a variety of different ways by one and the same body; and contrariwise, as one and the same thing can be affected in many ways, it can also in many different ways affect one and the same part of the body. Hence we can easily conceive that one and the same object may be the cause of many and conflicting emotions.

A man is as much affected pleasurably or painfully by the image of a thing past or future as by the image of a thing present.

I call a thing past or future, according as we either have been or shall be affected thereby. For instance, according as we have seen it, or are about to see it, according as it has recreated us, or will recreate us, according as it has harmed us, or will harm us. For, as we thus conceive it, we affirm its existence; that is, the body is affected by no emotion which excludes the existence of the thing, and therefore the body is affected by the image of the thing, in the same way as if the thing were actually present.

However, as it generally happens that those who have had many experiences, vacillate, so long as they regard a thing as future or past, and are usually in doubt about its issue; it follows that the emotions which arise from similar images of things are not so constant, but are generally disturbed by the images of other things, until men become assured of the issue. From what has just been said, we understand what is meant by the terms Hope, Fear, Confidence, Despair, Joy, and Disappointment. *Hope* is nothing else but *an inconstant pleasure, arising from the image of something future or past, whereof we do not yet know the issue. Fear,* on the other hand, is *an inconstant pain also arising from the image of something concerning which we are in doubt.* If the element of doubt be removed from these emotions, hope becomes *Confidence* and fear becomes *Despair.* In other words, *Pleasure or Pain arising from the image of something concerning which we have hoped or feared.* Again, *Joy* is *Pleasure arising from the image of something past whereof we doubted the issue. Disappointment* is the *Pain opposed to Joy.*

He who conceives that the object of his love is destroyed will feel pain; if he conceives that it is preserved he will feel pleasure.

He who conceives that the object of his hate is destroyed will feel pleasure.

He who conceives that the object of his love is affected pleasurably or painfully, will himself be affected pleasurably or painfully; and the one or the other emotion will be greater or less in the lover according as it is greater or less in the thing loved.

(*Pity* we may define as *pain arising from another's hurt.* What term we can use for pleasure arising from another's gain, I know not.)

If we conceive that anything pleasurably affects some object of our love, we shall be affected with love towards that thing. Contrariwise, if we conceive that it affects an object of our love painfully, we shall be affected with hatred toward it.

(We will call the *love toward him who confers a benefit on another, Approval;* and the *hatred toward*

him who injures another, we will call *Indignation.*
We must further remark that we not only feel pity
for a thing which we have loved, but also for a thing
which we have hitherto regarded without emotion,
provided that we deem that it resembles ourselves.
Thus, we bestow approval on one who has benefited
anything resembling ourselves, and, contrariwise,
are indignant with him who has done it an injury.)

He who conceives that an object of his hatred is
painfully affected, will feel pleasure. Contrariwise,
if he thinks that the said object is pleasurably affected, he will feel pain. Each of these emotions will
be greater or less, according as its contrary is greater
or less in the object of hatred.

If we conceive that anyone pleasurably affects an
object of our hate, we shall feel hatred toward him
also. If we conceive that he painfully affects the said
object, we shall feel love toward him.

Envy is nothing else but hatred, insofar as it is
regarded as disposing a man to rejoice in another's
hurt, and to grieve at another's advantage.

We endeavor to affirm, concerning ourselves, and
concerning what we love, everything that we conceive to affect pleasurably ourselves, or the loved
object. Contrariwise, we endeavor to negative everything which we conceive to affect painfully ourselves or our loved object.

We endeavor to affirm, concerning that which we hate, everything which we conceive to affect it painfully; and, contrariwise, we endeavor to deny, concerning it, everything which we conceive to affect it pleasurably.

A man may easily think too highly of himself, or a loved object, and, contrariwise, too meanly of a hated object. This feeling is called *pride*, in reference to the man who thinks too highly of himself, and is a species of madness, wherein a man dreams with his eyes open, thinking that he can accomplish all things that fall within the scope of his conception, and thereupon accounting them real, and exulting in them, so long as he is unable to conceive anything which excludes their existence and determines his own power of action. *Pride*, therefore is *pleasure springing from a man thinking too highly of himself*. Again, the *pleasure which arises from a man thinking too highly of another* is called *overesteem*. Whereas the *pleasure which arises from thinking too little of a man* is called *disdain*.

By the very fact that we conceive a thing which is like ourselves, and which we have not regarded with any emotion, to be affected with any emotion, we are ourselves affected with a like emotion. This imitation of emotion, when it is referred to pain, is called *compassion;* when it is referred to desire, it is called *emulation,* which is nothing else but *the desire of anything, engendered in us by the fact that we conceive that others have the like desire.*

If we conceive that anyone, whom we have hitherto regarded with no emotion, pleasurably affects something similar to ourselves, we shall be affected with love toward him. If, on the other hand, we conceive that he painfully affects the same, we shall be affected with hatred toward him.

We seek to free from misery, as far as we can, a thing we pity. This will or appetite for doing good, which arises from pity of the thing whereon we would confer a benefit, is called *benevolence,* and is nothing else but *desire arising from compassion.*

We endeavor to bring about whatsoever we concieve to conduce to pleasure; but we endeavor to remove or destroy whatsoever we conceive to be truly repugnant thereto, or to conduce to pain.

We shall endeavor to do whatsoever we conceive men to regard with pleasure, and contrariwise we shall shrink from doing that which we conceive men to shrink from. This endeavor to do a thing or leave it undone, solely in order to please men, we call *ambition,* especially when we so eagerly endeavor to please the vulgar, that we do or omit certain things to our own or another's hurt: in other cases it is generally called *kindliness.* Furthermore I give the name of *praise* to the *pleasure with which we conceive the action of another, whereby he has endeavored to please us;* but of *blame* to the *pain wherewith we feel aversion to his action.*

If anyone has done something which he conceives as affecting other men pleasurably, he will be affected by pleasure, accompanied by the idea of himself as cause; in other words, he will regard himself with pleasure. On the other hand, if he has done anything which he conceives as affecting others painfully, he will regard himself with pain.

As *love is pleasure accompanied by the idea of an external cause, and hatred is pain accompanied by the idea of an external cause,* the pleasure and pain in question will be a species of love and hatred. But, as the terms love and hatred are used in reference to external objects, we will employ other names for the emotions now under discussion: pleasure accompanied by the idea of an external cause we will style *Honor,* and the emotion contrary thereto we will style *Shame*—I mean in such cases as where pleasure or pain arises from a man's belief that he is being praised or blamed: otherwise pleasure accompanied by the idea of an external cause is called *self-complacency,* and its contrary pain is called *repentance.* Again, as it may happen that the pleasure, wherewith a man conceives that he affects others, may exist solely in his own imagination, and as everyone endeavors to conceive concerning himself that which he conceives will affect him with pleasure, it may easily come to pass that a vain man may be proud and may imagine that he is pleasing to all, when in reality he may be an annoyance to all.

If we conceive that anyone loves, desires, or hates anything which we ourselves love, desire, or hate, we shall thereupon regard the thing in question with more steadfast love, etc. On the contrary, if we think that anyone shrinks from something that we love, we shall undergo vaccilation of soul.

It follows that everyone endeavors, as far as possible, to cause others to love what he himself loves, and to hate what he himself hates: as the poet says: "As lovers let us share every hope and every fear: ironhearted were he who should love what the other leaves."

This endeavor to bring it about that our own likes and dislikes should meet with universal approval, is really ambition; wherefore we see that everyone by nature desires that the rest of mankind should live according to his own individual disposition: when such a desire is equally present in all, everyone stands in everyone else's way, and in wishing to be loved or praised by all, all become mutually hateful.

If we conceive that anyone takes delight in something, which only one person can possess, we shall endeavor to bring it about that the man in question shall not gain possession thereof.

We see that *man's nature is generally so constituted that he takes pity on those who fare ill, and envies those who fare well* with an amount of hatred proportioned to his own love for the goods in their possession. Further, we see that from the same property of human nature, whence it follows that men are merciful, it follows also that they are envious and ambitious. Lastly, if we make appeal to Experience, we shall find that she entirely confirms what we have said; more especially if we turn our attention to the first years of our life.

We find that children, whose body is continually, as it were, in equilibrium, laugh or cry simply because they see others laughing or crying; moreover, they desire forthwith to imitate whatever they see others doing, and to possess themselves whatever they conceive as delighting others: inasmuch as the images of things are, as we have said, modifications of the human body, or modes wherein the human body is affected and disposed by external causes to act in this or that manner.

When we love a thing similar to ourselves we endeavor, as far as we can, to bring about that it should love us in return.

The greater the emotion with which we conceive a loved object to be affected toward us, the greater will be our complacency.

If anyone conceives that an object of his love joins itself to another with closer bonds of friendship than he himself has attained to, he will be affected with hatred towards the loved object and with envy toward his rival.

Hatred toward an object of love joined with envy is called *Jealousy*, which accordingly is nothing else but a wavering of the disposition arising from combined love and hatred, accompanied by the idea of some rival who is envied. Further, this hatred toward the object of love will be greater, in proportion to the pleasure which the jealous man had been wont to derive from the reciprocated love of the said object; and also in proportion to the feelings he had previously entertained toward his rival. If he had hated him, he will forthwith hate the object of his love, because he conceives it is pleasurably affected by one whom he himself hates: and also because he is compelled to associate the image of his loved one with the image of him whom he hates.

This condition generally comes into play in the case of love for a woman: for he who thinks that a woman whom he loves gives herself to another will feel pain, not only because his own desire is restrained, but also because, being compelled to associate the image of her he loves with the parts of shame of another, he therefore shrinks from her.

We must add that a jealous man is not greeted by his beloved with the same joyful countenance as before, and this also gives him pain as a lover.

He who remembers a thing in which he has taken delight, desires to possess it under the same cirstances as when he first took delight therein.

Desire arising through pain or pleasure, hatred or love, is greater in proportion as the emotion is greater.

If a man has begun to hate an object of his love, so that love is thoroughly destroyed, he will, causes being equal, regard it with more hatred than if he had never loved it, and his hatred will be in proportion to the strength of his former love.

By *good* I mean every kind of pleasure, and all that conduces thereto, especially that which satisfies our longings, whatsoever they may be. By *evil*, I mean every kind of pain, especially that which frustrates our longings. We in no case desire a thing because we deem it good, but, contrariwise, we deem a thing good because we desire it: consequently we deem evil that which we shrink from; everyone, therefore, according to his particular emotions, judges or estimates what is good, what is bad, what is better, what is worse, and lastly, what is best, and what is worst. Thus a miser thinks that abundance of money is the best, and want of money the worst; an ambitious man desires nothing so much as glory, and fears nothing so much as shame. To an envious man nothing is more delightful than another's misfortune, and nothing more painful than another's success. So *every man, according to his emotions, judges a thing to be good or bad, useful or useless.* The emotion which induces a man to turn from that which he wishes, or to wish for that which he turns from, is called *timidity*, which may accordingly be defined as *the fear whereby a man is induced to avoid an evil which he regards as future by encountering a lesser evil.* But if the evil which he fears be shame, timidity becomes *bashfulness.* Lastly, if the desire to avoid a future evil be checked by the fear of another evil, so that the man knows not which to choose, fear becomes *consternation,* especially if both the evils feared be very great.

He who hates anyone will endeavor to do him an injury, unless he fears that a greater injury will thereby accrue to himself; on the other hand, he who loves anyone will, by the same law, seek to benefit him.

He who conceives himself to be hated by another, and believes that he has given him no cause for hatred, will hate that other in return.

He who conceives that one whom he loves hates him, will be a prey to conflicting hatred and love. For, insofar as he conceives that he is an object of hatred, he is determined to hate his enemy in return. But, by the hypothesis, he nevertheless loves him: whereby he will be a prey to conflicting hatred and love.

If a man conceives that one whom he has hitherto regarded without emotion, has done him any injury from motives of hatred, he will forthwith seek to repay the injury in kind.

The endeavor to injure one whom we hate is called *Anger;* the endeavor to repay in kind injury done to ourselves is called *Revenge.*

If anyone conceives that he is loved by another, and believes that he has given no cause for such love, he will love that other in return.

If he believes that he has given just cause for the love, he will take pride therein; this is what most often happens, and we said that its contrary took place whenever a man conceives himself to be hated by another. This reciprocal love, and consequently the desire of benefiting him who loves us, and who endeavors to benefit us, is called *gratitude* or *thankfulness.* It thus appears that men are much more prone to take vengeance than to return benefits.

He who imagines that he is loved by one whom he hates, will be a prey to conflicting hatred and love.

If hatred be the prevailing emotion, he will endeavor to injure him who loves him; this emotion is called *cruelty,* especially if the victim be believed to have given no ordinary cause for hatred.

He who has conferred a benefit on anyone from motives of love or honor will feel pain, if he sees that the benefit is received without gratitude.

Hatred is increased by being reciprocated, and can on the other hand be destroyed by love.

Hatred which is completely vanquished by love passes into love: and love is thereupon greater than if hatred had not preceded it.

Though this be so, no one will endeavor to hate anything, or to be affected with pain, for the sake of enjoying this greater pleasure; that is, no one will desire that he should be injured, in the hope of recovering from the injury, nor long to be ill for the sake of getting well. For everyone will always endeavor to persist in his being, and to ward off pain as far as he can. If the contrary is conceivable, namely, that a man should desire to hate someone, in order that he might love him the more thereafter, he will always desire to hate him.

For the strength of the love is in proportion to the strength of the hatred, wherefore the man would desire that the hatred be continually increased more and more, and, for a similar reason, he would desire to become more and more ill, in order that he might take a greater pleasure in being restored to health: in such a case he would always endeavor to be ill, which is absurd.

If a man conceives that anyone similar to himself

hates anything also similar to himself, which he loves, he will hate that person.

If a man has been affected pleasurably or painfully by anyone of a class or nation different from his own, and if the pleasure or pain has been accompanied by the idea of the said stranger as cause, under the general category of the class or nation: the man will feel love or hatred, not only to the individual stranger, but also to the whole class or nation whereto he belongs.

Joy arising from the fact that anything we hate is destroyed, or suffers other injury, is never unaccompanied by a certain pain in us.

Love or hatred toward, for instance, Peter is destroyed, if the pleasure involved in the former, or the pain involved in the latter emotion, be associated with the idea of another cause: and will be diminished in proportion as we conceive Peter not to have been the sole cause of either emotion.

Love or hatred toward a thing, which we conceive to be free, must, other conditions being similar, be greater than if it were felt toward a thing acting by necessity.

Hence it follows, that men, thinking themselves to be free, feel more love or hatred toward one another than toward anything else.

Anything whatever can be, accidentally, a cause of hope or fear.

Things which are accidentally the causes of hope or fear are called good or evil omens. Now, insofar as such omens are the cause of hope or fear, they are the causes also of pleasure and pain; consequently we, to this extent, regard them with love or hatred, and endeavor either to invoke them as means toward that which we hope for, or to remove them as obstacles, or causes of that which we fear. It follows, further, that we are naturally so constituted as to believe readily in that which we hope for, and with difficulty in that which we fear; moreover, we are apt to estimate such objects above or below their true value. Hence there have arisen superstitions, whereby men are everywhere assailed.

However, I do not think it worth while to point out here the vacillations springing from hope and fear; it follows from the definition of these emotions, that there can be no hope without fear, and no fear without hope, as I will duly explain in the proper place. Further, insofar as we hope for or fear anything, we regard it with love or hatred; thus everyone can apply by himself to hope and fear what we have said concerning love and hatred.

Different men may be differently affected by the same object, and the same man may be differently affected at different times by the same object.

We see that it is possible that what one man loves another may hate, and that what one man fears another may not fear; or, again, that one and the same man may love what he once hated, or may be bold where he once was timid, and so on. Again, as everyone judges according to his emotions what is good, what bad, what better, and what worse, it follows that men's judgements may vary no less than their emotions, hence when we compare some with others, we distinguish them solely by the diversity of their emotions, and style some intrepid, others timid, others by some other epithet.

For instance, I shall call a man *intrepid* if he despises an evil which I am accustomed to fear; if I further take into consideration that, in his desire to injure his enemies and to benefit those whom he loves, he is not restrained by the fear of an evil · which is sufficient to restrain me, I shall call him *daring*.

Again, a man will appear *timid* to me if he fears an evil which I am accustomed to despise; and if I further take into consideration that his desire is restrained by the fear of an evil, which is not sufficient to restrain me, I shall say that he is *cowardly;* and in like manner will everyone pass judgement.

Lastly, from this inconstancy in the nature of human judgement, inasmuch as a man often judges of things solely by his emotions, and inasmuch as the things which he believes cause pleasure or pain, and therefore endeavors to promote or prevent, are often purely imaginary, we may readily conceive that a man may be at one time affected with pleasure, and at another with pain, accompanied by the idea of himself as cause.

Thus we can easily understand what are *Repentance* and *Self-complacency*. *Repentance is pain, accompanied by the idea of one's self as cause; Self-complacency is pleasure accompanied by the idea of one's self as cause,* and these emotions are most intense because men believe themselves to be free.

An object which we have formerly seen in conjunction with others, and which we do not conceive to have any property that is not common to many, will not be regarded by us for so long as an object which we conceive to have some property peculiar to itself.

The mental modification, or imagination of a particular thing, insofar as it is alone in the mind, is called *Wonder;* but if it be excited by an object of fear, it is called *Consternation,* because wonder at an evil keeps a man so engrossed in the simple contemplation thereof that he has no power to think of anything else whereby he might avoid the evil. If, however, the object of wonder be a man's prudence, industry, or anything of that sort, inasmuch as the said man is thereby regarded as far surpassing ourselves, wonder is called *Veneration;* otherwise, if a man's anger, envy, etc., be what we wonder at, the emotion is called *Horror.* Again, if it be the prudence, industry, or what not, of a man we love, that we wonder at, our love will on this account be the greater, and when joined to wonder or veneration is called *Devotion*. We may in like manner conceive hatred, hope, confidence, and the other emotions, as associated with wonder; and we should thus be able to deduce more emotions than those which have obtained names in ordinary spech. Whence it is evident that the names of the emotions have been applied in accordance rather with their ordinary manifestations than with an accurate knowledge of their nature.

To wonder is opposed *Contempt,* which generally arises from the fact that, because we see someone wondering at, loving, or fearing something, or because something, at first sight, appears to be like things which we ourselves wonder at, love, fear, etc., we are, in consequence, determined to wonder at, love, or fear that thing. But if from the presence, or more accurate contemplation of the said thing, we are compelled to deny concerning it all that can be the cause of wonder, love, fear, etc., the mind then, by the presence of the thing, remains determined to think rather of those qualities which are not in it, than of those which are in it; whereas, on the other hand, the presence of the object would cause it more particularly to regard that which is therein.

As devotion springs from wonder at a thing which we love, so does *Derision* spring from contempt of a thing which we hate or fear, and *Scorn* from contempt of folly, as veneration from wonder at prudence. Lastly, we can conceive the emotions of love, hope, honor, etc., in association with contempt, and can thence deduce other emotions, which are not distinguished one from another by any recognized name.

When the mind regards itself and its own power of activity, it feels pleasure: and that pleasure is greater in proportion to the distinctness wherewith it conceives itself and its own power of activity.

The mind endeavors to conceive only such things as assert its power of activity.

When the mind contemplates its own weakness, it feels pain thereat. This pain is more and more fostered if a man conceives that he is blamed by others.

Pain, accompanied by the idea of our own weakness, is called *humility;* the pleasure which springs from the contemplation of ourselves is called *self-love* or *self-complacency*. And inasmuch as this feeling is renewed as often as a man contemplates his own virtues, or his own power of activity, it follows that everyone is fond of narrating his own exploits, and displaying the force both of his body and mind, and also that, for this reason, men are troublesome one to another. Again, it follows that men are naturally envious, rejoicing in the shortcomings of their equals, and feeling pain at their virtues. For whenever a man conceives his own actions, he is affected with pleasure, in proportion as his actions display more perfection, and he conceives them more distinctly—that is, in proportion as he can distinguish them from others, and regard them as something special.

Therefore, a man will take most pleasure in contemplating himself when he contemplates some quality which he denies to others. But, if that which he affirms of himself be attributable to the idea of man or animals in general, he will not be so greatly pleased: he will, on the contrary, feel pain if he conceives that his own actions fall short when compared with those of others. This pain he will endeavor to remove, by putting a wrong construction on the actions of his equals, or by, as far as he can, embellishing his own.

It is thus apparent that men are naturally prone to hatred and envy, which latter is fostered by their education. For parents are accustomed to incite their children to virtue solely by the spur of honor and envy.

No one envies the virtue of anyone who is not his equal.

We venerate a man, through wonder at his prudence, fortitude, etc., because we conceive those qualities to be peculiar to him, and not as common to our nature; we, therefore, no more envy their possessor than we envy trees for being tall, or lions for being courageous.

There are as many kinds of pleasure, of pain, of desire, and of every emotion compounded of these, such as vacillations of spirit, or derived from these, such as love, hatred, hope, fear, etc., as there are kinds of objects whereby we are affected.

Among the kinds of emotions, the chief are *luxury, drunkenness, lust, avarice,* and *ambition,* being merely species of love or desire, displaying the nature of those emotions in a manner varying according to the object with which they are concerned. For by luxury, drunkenness, lust, avarice, ambition, etc., we simply mean the immoderate love of feasting, drinking, venery, riches, and fame. Furthermore, these emotions, insofar as we distinguish them from others merely by the objects wherewith they are concerned, have no contraries. For *temperance, sobriety,* and *chastity,* which we are wont to oppose to luxury, drunkennesss, and lust, are not emotions or passive states, but indicate a power of the mind which moderates the last-named emotions.

However, I cannot here explain the remaining kinds of emotions (seeing that they are as numerous as the kinds of objects), nor, if I could, would it be necessary. It is sufficient for our purpose, namely, to determine the strength of the emotions, and the mind's power over them, to have a general definition

of each emotion. It is sufficient, I repeat, to understand the general properties of the emotions and the
mind, to enable us to determine the quality and extent of the mind's power in moderating and checking
the emotions. Thus, though there is a great difference between various emotions of love, hatred, or
desire—for instance, between love felt toward children and love felt toward a wife—there is no need
for us to take cognizance of such differences, or
to track out further the nature and origin of the
emotions.

Any emotion of a given individual differs from the
emotion of another individual, only insofar as the
essence of one individual differs from the essence
of the other.

Hence it follows that the emotions of the animals
which are called irrational (for after learning the
origin of mind we cannot doubt that brutes feel)
only differ from man's emotions to the extent that
brute nature differs from human nature. Horse and
man are alike carried away by the desire of pro-
creation; but the desire of the former is equine, the
desire of the latter is human. So also the lusts and
appetites of insects, fishes, and birds must needs
vary according to the several natures.

Thus, although each individual lives content and
rejoices in that nature belonging to him wherein
he has his being, yet the life wherein each is content and rejoices is nothing else but the idea, or
soul, of the said individual, and hence the joy of

one only differs in nature from the joy of another.

Lastly, it follows from the foregoing proposition, that there is no small difference between the joy which actuates, say, a drunkard, and the joy possessed by a philosopher, as I just mention here by the way.

Thus far I have treated of the emotions attributable to man, insofar as he is passive. It remains to add a few words on those attributable to him insofar as he is active.

Besides pleasure and desire, which are passivities or passions, there are other emotions derived from pleasure and desire which are attributable to us insofar as we are active.

Among all the emotions attributable to the mind as active, there are none which cannot be referred to pleasure or pain.

All actions following from emotion, which are attributable to the mind in virtue of its understanding, I set down to strength of character, which I divide into courage and highmindedness. By courage I mean the desire whereby every man strives to preserve his own being in accordance solely with the dictates of reason. By highmindedness I mean the desire whereby every man endeavors, solely under the dictates of reason, to aid other men and to unite them to himself in friendship. Those actions, therefore, which have regard solely to the good of the agent I set down to courage, those which aim at the good of others I set down to highmindedness. Thus temperance, sobriety, and presence of mind in danger, etc., are varieties of courage; courtesy, mercy, etc., are varieties of highmindedness.

I think I have thus explained, and displayed through their primary causes the principal emotions and vacillations of spirit, which arise from the combinations of the three primary emotions, to wit, desire, pleasure, and pain. It is evident from what I have said, that we are in many ways driven about by external causes, and that like waves of the sea driven by contrary winds we toss to and fro unwitting of the issue and of our fate. But I have said that I have only set forth the chief conflicting emotions, not all that might be given. For, by proceeding in the same way as above, we can easily show that love is united to repentance, scorn, shame, etc. I think everyone will agree from what has been said, that the emotions may be compounded one with another in so many ways, and so many variations may arise therefrom, as to exceed all possibility of computation. However, for my purpose, it is enough to have enumerated the most important; to reckon up the rest which I have omitted would be more curious than profitable. It remains to remark concerning love, that it very often happens that while we are enjoying a thing which we longed for, the body, from the act of enjoyment, acquires a new disposition whereby it is determined in another way: other images of things are aroused in it, and the mind begins to conceive and desire something fresh.

For example, when we conceive something which generally delights us with its flavor, we desire to enjoy, that is, to eat it. But whilst we are thus enjoying it, the stomach is filled and the body is otherwise disposed. If, therefore, when the body is thus otherwise disposed, the image of the food which is present be stimulated and consequently the endeavor or desire to eat it be stimulated also, the new disposition of the body will feel repugnance to the desire or attempt, and consequently the presence of the food which we formerly longed for will become odious.

This revulsion of feeling is called satiety or weariness. For the rest, I have neglected the outward modifications of the body observable in emotions, such, for instance, as trembling, pallor, sobbing, laughter, etc., for these are attributable to the body only, without any reference to the mind. Lastly, the definitions of the emotions require to be supplemented in a few points; I will therefore repeat them, interpolating such observations as I think should here and there be added.

Desire is the actual essence of man, insofar as it is conceived as determined to a particular activity by some given modification of itself.

Pleasure is the transition of a man from a less to a greater perfection.

Pain is the transition of a man from a greater to a less perfection.

Wonder is the conception of anything, wherein the mind comes to a stand, because the particular concept in question has no connection with other concepts.

I recognize only three primitive or primary emotions, namely, pleasure, pain, and desire. I have spoken of wonder, simply because it is customary to speak of certain emotions springing from the three primitive ones by different names, when they are referred to the objects of our wonder. I am led by the same motive to add a definition of contempt.

Contempt is the conception of anything which touches the mind so little that its presence leads the mind to imagine those qualities which are not in it rather than such as are in it.

Love is pleasure, accompanied by the idea of an external cause.

Hatred is pain, accompanied by the idea of an external cause.

Inclination is pleasure, accompanied by the idea of something which is accidentally a cause of pleasure.

Aversion is pain, accompanied by the idea of something which is accidentally the cause of pain.

Devotion is love toward one whom we admire

Derision is pleasure arising from our conceiving the presence of a quality which we despise in an object which we hate.

Hope is an inconstant pleasure, arising from the idea of something past or future, whereof we to a certain extent doubt the issue.

Fear is an inconstant pain arising from the idea of something past or future, whereof we to a certain extent doubt the issue.

Confidence is pleasure arising from the idea of something past or future, wherefrom all cause of doubt has been removed.

Despair is pain arising from the idea of something past or future, wherefrom all cause of doubt has been removed.

Joy is pleasure accompanied by the idea of something past, which has had an issue beyond our hope.

Disappointment is pain accompanied by the idea of something past, which has had an issue contrary to our hope.

Pity is pain accompanied by the idea of evil, which has befallen someone else whom we conceive to be like ourselves.

Approval is love toward one who has done good to another.

Indignation is hatred toward one who has done evil to another.

Partiality is thinking too highly of anyone because of the love we bear him.

Disparagement is thinking too meanly of anyone, because we hate him.

Envy is hatred, insofar as it induces a man to be pained by another's good fortune, and to rejoice in another's evil fortune.

Sympathy is love, insofar as it induces a man to feel pleasure at another's good fortune, and pain at another's evil fortune.

Self-approval is pleasure arising from a man's contemplation of himself and his own power of action.

Humility is pain arising from a man's contemplation of his own weakness of body or mind.

Repentance is pain accompanied by the idea of some action which we believe we have performed by the decision of our mind.

Pride is thinking too highly of one's self from self-love.

Self-abasement is thinking too meanly of one's self by reason of pain.

Honor is pleasure accompanied by the idea of some action of our own, which we believe to be praised by others.

Shame is pain accompanied by the idea of some action of our own, which we believe to be blamed by others.

Regret is the desire or appetite to possess something, kept alive by the remembrance of the said thing, and at the same time constrained by the remembrance of other things which exclude the existence of it.

Emulation is the desire of something, engendered in us by our conception that others have the same desire.

Thankfulness or Gratitude is the desire or zeal springing from love, whereby we endeavor to benefit him who, with similar feelings of love, has conferred a benefit on us.

Benevolence is the desire of benefiting one whom we pity.

Anger is the desire whereby through hatred we are induced to injure one whom we hate.

Revenge is the desire whereby we are induced, through mutual hatred, to injure one who, with similar feelings, has injured us.

Cruelty or savageness is the desire whereby a man is impelled to injure one whom we love or pity.

Daring is the desire whereby a man is sent on to do something dangerous which his equals fear to attempt.

Cowardice is attributed to one whose desire is checked by the fear of some danger which his equals dare to encounter.

Timidity is the desire to avoid a greater evil, which we dread, by undergoing a lesser evil.

Consternation is attributed to one whose desire of avoiding evil is checked by amazement at the evil which he fears.

Courtesy, or deference, is the desire of acting in a way that should please men, and refraining from that which should displease them.

Ambition is the immoderate desire of power.

Luxury is excessive desire, or even love of living sumptuously.

Intemperance is the excessive desire and love of drinking.

Avarice is the excessive desire and love of riches.

Lust is desire and love in the matter of sexual intercourse. (Whether this desire be excessive or not, it is still called lust.)

Again, I have already pointed out that temperance, sobriety, and chastity indicate rather a power than a passivity of the mind. It may, nevertheless, happen that an avaricious, an ambitious, or a timid man may abstain from excess in eating, drinking, or sexual indulgence, yet avarice, ambition, and fear are not contraries to luxury, drunkenness, and debauchery. For an avaricious man often is glad to gorge himself with food and drink at another man's expense.

An ambitious man will restrain himself in nothing, so long as he thinks his indulgences are secret; and if he lives among drunkards and debauchees, he will, from the mere fact of being ambitious, be more prone to those vices. Lastly, a timid man does that which he would not.

For though an avaricious man should, for the sake of avoiding death, cast his riches into the sea, he will nonetheless remain avaricious; so, also, if a lustful man is downcast, because he cannot follow his bent, he does not, on the ground of abstention, cease to be lustful. In fact, these emotions are not so much concerned with the actual feasting, drinking, etc., as with the appetite and love of such. Nothing, therefore, can be opposed to these emotions, but high-mindedness and valor, whereof I will speak presently.

The definitions of jealousy and other waverings of the mind I pass over in silence, first, because they arise from the compounding of the emotions already described; secondly, because many of them have no distinctive names, which shows that it is sufficient for practical purposes to have merely a general knowledge of them.

However, it is established from the definitions of the emotions, which we have set forth, that they all spring from desire, pleasure, or pain, or, rather, that there is nothing besides these three; wherefore each is wont to be called by a variety of names in accordance with its various relations and extrinsic tokens. If we now direct our attention to these primitive emotions, and to what has been said concerning the nature of the mind, we shall be able thus to define the emotions, insofar as they are referred to the mind only.

Emotion, which is called a passivity of the soul, is a confused idea, whereby the mind affirms concerning its body, or any part thereof, a force for existence greater or less than before, and by the presence of which the mind is determined to think of one thing rather than another.

And inasmuch as the essence of mind consists in the fact that it affirms the actual existence of its own body, and inasmuch as we understand by perfection the very essence of a thing, it follows that the mind passes to greater or less perfection when it happens to affirm concerning its own body, or any part thereof, something involving more or less reality than before.

When, therefore, I say that the power of the mind is increased or diminished, I merely mean that the mind has formed of its own body, or of some part thereof, an idea involving more or less of reality, than it had already affirmed concerning its own body. For the excellence of ideas, and the actual power of thinking are measured by the excellence of the object.

On Human Bondage

or,

The Power of Desires

Perfection,
the Good, and the Bad

Human infirmity in moderating and checking the emotions I name *bondage:* for, *when a man is a prey of his emotions, he is not his own master, but lies at the mercy of fortune:* so much so, that he is often compelled, while seeing that which is better for him, to follow that which is worse. Why this is so, and what is good or evil in the emotions, I propose to show in this part of my treatise. But, before I begin, it would be well to make a few prefatory observations on perfection and imperfection, good and evil.

When a man has purposed to make a given thing, and has brought it to perfection, his work will be pronounced perfect, not only by himself, but by everyone who rightly knows, or thinks that he knows, the intention and aim of its author.

For instance, suppose anyone sees a work (which I assume to be not yet completed), and knows that the aim of the author of that work is to build a house, he will call the work imperfect; he will, on the other hand, call it perfect as soon as he sees that it is carried through to the end which its author had purposed for it. But if a man sees a work, the like whereof he has never seen before, and if he knows not the intention of the artificer, he plainly cannot know whether that work be perfect or imperfect. Such seems to be the primary meaning of these terms.

But, after men began to form general ideas, to think out types of houses, buildings, towers, etc., and to prefer certain types to others, it came about that each man called perfect that which he saw agree with the general idea he had formed of the thing in question, and called imperfect that which he saw agree less with his own preconceived type, even though it had evidently been completed in accordance with the idea of its artificer. This seems to be the only reason for calling natural phenomena, which, indeed, are not made with human hands, perfect or imperfect: for men are wont to form general ideas of things natural, no less than of things artificial, and such ideas they hold as types, believing that Nature (who they think does nothing without an object) has them in view, and has set them as types before herself. Therefore, when they behold something in Nature which does not wholly conform to the preconceived type which they have formed of the thing in question, they say that Nature has fallen short or has blundered, and has left her work incomplete.

Thus we see that men are wont to style natural

phenomena prefect or imperfect rather from their own prejudices, than from true knowledge of what they pronounce upon.

Now we know that *Nature does not work with an end in view.* For the eternal and infinite Being, which we call God or Nature, acts by the same necessity as that whereby it exists. For we can see that by the same necessity of its nature, whereby it exists, it likewise works. The reason or cause why God or Nature exists, and the reason why He acts, are one and the same.

Therefore, as He does not exist for the sake of an end, so neither does He act for the sake of an end; of His existence and of His action there is neither origin nor end. Wherefore, a cause which is called final is nothing else but human desire, insofar as it is considered as the origin or cause of anything. For example, when we say that to be inhabited is the final cause of this or that house, we mean nothing more than that a man, conceiving the conveniences of household life, had a desire to build a house. Wherefore, the being inhabited, insofar as it is regarded as a final cause, is nothing else but this particular desire, which is really the efficient cause; it is regarded as the primary cause, because men are generally ignorant of the causes of their desires.

They are, as I have often said already, conscious of their own actions and appetites, but ignorant of the causes whereby they are determined to any particular desire.

Perfection and imperfection, then, are in reality merely modes of thinking, or notions which we form from a comparison among one another of individuals of the same species; hence I said above that by reality and perfection I mean the same thing. For we are wont to refer all the individual things in nature to one genus, which is called the highest genus, namely, to the category of Being, whereto absolutely all individuals in nature belong.

Thus, insofar as we refer the individuals in nature to this category, and comparing them one with another, find that some possess more of being or reality than others, we, to this extent, say that some are more perfect than others. Again, insofar as we attribute to them anything implying negation—as term, end, infirmity, etc.—we, to this extent, call them imperfect, because they do not affect our mind so much as the things which we call perfect, not because they have any intrinsic deficiency, or because Nature has blundered. For nothing lies within the scope of a thing's nature, save that which follows from the necessity of the nature of its efficient cause necessarily comes to pass.

As for the terms good and bad, they indicate no positive quality in things regarded in themselves, but are merely modes of thinking, or notions which we form from the comparison of things one with another. *Thus one and the same thing can be at the same time good, bad, and indifferent.* For instance, music is good for him that is melancholy, bad for him that mourns; for him that is deaf, it is neither good nor bad.

Nevertheless, though this be so, the terms should still be retained. For, inasmuch as we desire to form an idea of man as a type of human nature which we may hold in view, it will be useful for us to retain the terms in question, in the sense I have indicated. In what follows, then, I shall mean by "good" that which we certainly know to be a means of approaching more nearly to the type of human nature which we have set before ourselves; by "bad," that which we certainly know to be a hindrance to us in approaching the said type.

Again, we shall say that men are more perfect, or more imperfect, in proportion as they approach more or less nearly to the said type. For it must be specially remarked that, when I say that a man passes from a lesser to a greater perfection, or vice versa, I do not mean that he is changed from one essence or reality to another; for instance, a horse would be as completely destroyed by being changed into a man, as by being changed into an insect. What I mean is that we conceive the thing's power of action, insofar as this is understood by its nature, to be increased or diminished.

Lastly, by perfection in general I shall, as I have said, mean reality—in other words, each thing's essence, insofar as it exists, and operates in a particular manner, and without paying any regard to its duration. For no given thing can be said to be more perfect because it has passed a longer time in existence. The duration of things cannot be determined by their essence, for the essence of things involves no fixed and definite period of existence; but everything, whether it be more perfect or less perfect, will always be able to persist in existence with the same force wherewith it began to exist; wherefore, in this respect, all things are equal.

The Force
of Passion

No positive quality possessed by a false idea is removed by the presence of what is true, in virtue of its being true.

For instance, when we look at the sun, we conceive that it is distant from us about two hundred feet; in this judgment we err, so long as we are in ignorance of its true distance; when its true distance is known, the error is removed, but not imagination; or, in other words, the idea of the sun, which only explains the nature of the luminary, insofar as the body is affected thereby: wherefore, though we know the real distance, we shall still nevertheless imagine the sun to be near us.

For we do not imagine the sun to be so near us because we are ignorant of its true distance, but because the mind conceives the magnitude of the sun to the extent that the body is affected thereby. Thus, when the rays of the sun falling on the surface of the water are reflected into our eyes, we imagine the sun as if it were in the water, though we are aware of its real position; and similarly other imaginations, wherein the mind is deceived, whether they indicate the natural disposition of the body, or that its power of activity is increased or diminished, are not contrary to the truth, and do not vanish at its presence.

It happens indeed that, when we mistakenly fear an evil, the fear vanishes when we hear the true tidings; but the contrary also happens, namely, that we fear an evil which will certainly come, and our fear vanishes when we hear false tidings; thus imaginations do not vanish at the presence of the truth, in virtue of its being true, but because other imaginations, stronger than the first, supervene and exclude the present existence of that which we imagined.

We are only passive insofar as we are a part of nature, which cannot be conceived by itself without other parts.

The force whereby a man persists in existing is limited, and is infinitely surpassed by the power of external causes.

It is impossible that man should not be a part of Nature, or that he should be capable of undergoing no changes, save such as can be understood through his nature only as their adequate cause.

Man is necessarily always a prey to his passions, he follows and obeys the general order of nature, and he accommodates himself thereto, as much as the nature of things demands.

The power and increase of every passion, and its persistence in existing are not defined by the power whereby we ourselves endeavor to persist in existing, but by the power of an external cause compared with our own.

The force of any passion or emotion can overcome the rest of a man's activities or power, so that the emotion becomes obstinately fixed to him.

An emotion can only be controlled or destroyed by another emotion contrary thereto, and with more power for controlling emotion.

An emotion, insofar as it is referred to the mind, can only by controlled or destroyed through an idea of a modification of the body contrary to, and stronger than, that which we are undergoing. For the emotion which we undergo can only be checked or destroyed by an emotion contrary to, and stronger than, itself, in other words, only by an idea of a modification of the body contrary to, and stronger than, the modification which we undergo.

An emotion, whereof we conceive the cause to be with us at the present time, is stronger than if we did not conceive the cause to be with us.

We are affected by the image of what is past or future with the same emotion as if the thing conceived were present. This is only true insofar as we look solely to the image of the thing in question itself; for the thing's nature is unchanged, whether we have conceived it or not; I do not deny that the image becomes weaker, when we regard as present to us other things which exclude the present existence of the future object.

The image of something past or future, that is, of a thing which we regard as in relation to time past or time future, to the exclusion of time present, is, when other conditions are equal, weaker than the image of something present; consequently an emotion felt toward what is past or future is less intense, other conditions being equal, than an emotion felt toward something present.

Toward something future, which we conceive as close at hand, we are affected more intensely than if we conceive that its time for existence is separated from the present by a longer interval; so too by the remembrance of what we conceive to have not long passed away we are affected more intensely than if we conceive that it has long passed away.

An emotion toward that which we conceive as necessary is, when other conditions are equal, more intense than an emotion toward that which is possible, or contingent, or non-necessary.

An emotion toward a thing which we know not to exist at the present time, and which we conceive as possible, is more intense, other conditions being equal, than an emotion toward a thing contingent.

An emotion toward a thing which we know not to exist in the present, and which we conceive as contingent, is far fainter than if we conceive the thing to be present with us.

Emotion toward a thing contingent, which we know not to exist in the present, is, other conditions being equal, fainter than an emotion toward a thing past.

The knowledge of good and evil is nothing else but the emotions of pleasure or pain, insofar as we are conscious thereof.

A true knowledge of good and evil cannot check any emotion by virtue of being true, but only insofar as it is considered as an emotion.

Desire arising from the knowledge of good and bad can be quenched or checked by many of the other desires arising from the emotions whereby we are assailed.

Desire arising from the knowledge of good and evil, insofar as such knowledge regards what is future, may be more easily controlled or quenched than the desire for what is agreeable at the present moment.

Desire arising from the true knowledge of good and evil, insofar as such knowledge is concerned with what is contingent, can be controlled far more easily still than desire for things that are present.

I think I have now shown the reason why men are moved by opinion more readily than by true reason, why it is that the true knowledge of good and evil stirs up conflicts in the soul, and often yields to every kind of passion. This state of things gave rise to the exclamation of the poet:

> "The better path I gaze at and approve
> The worse—I follow."

Ecclesiastes seems to have had the same thought in his mind, when he says, "He who increaseth knowledge increaseth sorrow." I have not written the above with the object of drawing the conclusion that ignorance is more excellent than knowledge, or that a wise man is on a par with a fool in controlling his emotions, but because it is necessary to know the power and the infirmity of our nature, before we can determine what reason can do in restraining the emotions, and what is beyond her power.

Desire arising from pleasure is, other conditions being equal, stronger than desire arising from pain.

Piety and
Selfishness

In these few remarks I have talked of the causes of human infirmity and inconstancy, and why men do not abide by the precepts of reason. It now remains for me to point out what course is marked out for us by reason, which of the emotions are in harmony with the rules of human reason, and which of them are contrary thereto.

As reason makes no demands contrary to nature, it demands that every man should love himself, should seek that which is useful to him—I mean, that which is really useful to him: he should desire everything which really brings man to greater perfection—and should, each for himself, endeavor as far as he can to preserve his own being. This is as necessarily true as that a whole is greater than its part.

Again, as virtue is nothing else but action in accordance with the laws of one's own nature, and as no one endeavors to preserve his own being except in accordance with the laws of his own nature, it follows, first, that the foundation of virtue is the endeavor to preserve one's own being, and that happiness consists in man's power of preserving his own being; secondly, that virtue is to be desired for its own sake, and that there is nothing more excellent or more useful to us, for the sake of which we should desire it; thirdly and lastly, that suicides are weak-minded, and are overcome by external causes repugnant to their nature.

Further, it follows that we can never arrive at doing without all external things for the preservation of our being or living, so as to have no relations with things which are outside ourselves. Again, if we consider our mind, we see that our intellect would be more imperfect if mind were alone, and could understand nothing besides itself. There are, then, many things outside ourselves which are useful to us, and are, therefore, to be desired.

Of such none can be discerned more excellent than those which are in entire agreement with our nature. For if, for example, two individuals of entirely the same nature are united, they form a combination twice as powerful as either of them singly.

Therefore, *to man there is nothing more useful than man*—nothing, I repeat, more excellent for preserving their being can be wished for by men than that all should so in all points agree that the minds and bodies of all should form, as it were, one single mind and one single body, and that all should, with one consent, as far as they are able, endeavor to preserve their being, and all with one consent seek what is useful to them all. Hence, men who are governed by reason—that is, who seek what is useful to them in accordance with reason—desire for themselves nothing which they do not also desire for the rest of mankind, and, consequently, are just, faithful, and honorable in their conduct.

Such are the dictates of reason, which I purposed thus briefly to indicate, before beginning to prove them in greater detail. I have taken this course in order, if possible, to gain the attention of those who believe that the principle that every man is bound to seek what is useful for himself is the foundation of impiety, rather than of piety and virtue.

Man Is
to Man a God

Every man, by the laws of his nature, necessarily desires or shrinks from that which he deems to be good or bad.

The more every man endeavors, and is able to seek what is useful to him—in other words, to preserve his own being—the more is he endowed with virtue; on the contrary, in proportion as a man neglects to seek what is useful to him, that is, to preserve his own being, he is wanting in power.

No one neglects seeking his own good, or preserving his own being, unless he be overcome by causes external and foreign to his nature. No one, I say, from the necessity of his own nature, or otherwise than under compulsion from external causes, shrinks from food, or kills himself: which latter may be done in a variety of ways.

A man, for instance, kills himself under the compulsion of another man, who twists round his right hand, wherewith he happened to have taken up a sword, and forces him to turn the blade against his own heart; or again, he may be compelled, like

Seneca, by a tyrant's command, to open his own veins—that is, to escape a greater evil by incurring a lesser; or, lastly, latent external causes may so disorder his imagination, and so affect his body, that it may assume a nature contrary to its former one, and whereof the idea cannot exist in the mind.

But that a man, from the necessity of his own nature, should endeavor to become nonexistent, is as impossible as that something should be made out of nothing, as everyone will see for himself, after a little reflection.

No one can desire to be blessed, to act rightly, and to live rightly, without at the same time wishing to be, to act, and to live—in other words, to actually exist.

No virtue can be conceived as prior to this endeavor to preserve one's own being.

The effort for self-preservation is the first and only foundation of virtue. For prior to this principle nothing can be conceived, and without it no virtue can be conceived.

To act absolutely in obedience to virtue is in us the same thing as to act, to live, or to preserve one's being (these three terms are identical in meaning) in accordance with the dictates of reason on the basis of seeking what is useful to one's self.

No one wishes to preserve his being for the sake of anything else.

Man, insofar as he is determined to a particular action because he has inadequate ideas, cannot be absolutely said to act in obedience to virtue; he can only be so described insofar as he is determined for the action because he understands.

Whatsoever we endeavor in obedience to reason is nothing further than to understand; neither does the mind, insofar as it makes use of reason, judge anything to be useful to it, save such things as are conducive to understanding.

We know nothing to be certainly good or evil, save such things as really conduce to understanding, or such as are able to hinder us from understanding.

The mind's highest good is the knowledge of God, and the mind's highest virtue is to know God.

No individual thing which is entirely different from our own nature, can help or check our power activity, and absolutely nothing can do us good or harm, unless it has something in common with our nature.

A thing cannot be bad for us through the quality which it has in common with our nature, but it is bad for us insofar as it contrary to our nature.

Insofar as a thing is in harmony with our nature, it is necessarily good.

It follows, that, in proportion as a thing is in harmony with our nature, so it is more useful or better for us, and vice versa, in proportion as a thing is more useful for us, so is it more in harmony with our nature. For, insofar as it is not in harmony with our nature, it will necessarily be different therefrom or contrary thereto.

If different, it can neither be good nor bad; if contrary, it will be contrary to that which is in harmony with our nature, that is, contrary to what is good—in short, bad. Nothing, therefore, can be good, except insofar as it in harmony with our nature; and hence a thing is useful, in proportion as it is in harmony with our nature, and vice versa.

Insofar as men are a prey to passion, they cannot, in that respect, be said to be naturally in harmony.

Men can differ in nature, insofar as they are assailed by those emotions, which are passions, or passive states; and to this extent one and the same man is variable and inconstant.

Insofar as men are assailed by emotions which are passions, they can be contrary one to another.

Insofar only as men live in obedience to reason, do they always necessarily agree in nature.

There is no individual thing in nature, which is more useful to man, than a man who lives in obedience to reason. For that thing is to man most useful, which is most in harmony with his nature; that is, obviously, man. But man acts absolutely according to the laws of his nature, when he lives in obedience to reason, and to this extent only is always necessarily in harmony with the nature of another man; wherefore among individual things *nothing is more useful to man, than a man who lives in obedience to reason.*

As every man seeks most that which is useful to him, so are men most useful one to another. For the more a man seeks what is useful to him and endeavors to preserve himself, the more is he endowed with virtue, or, what is the same thing, the more he is endowed with power to act according to the laws of his nature, that is to live in obedience to reason. But men are most in natural harmony when they live in obedience to reason; therefore men will be most useful one to another when each seeks most that which is useful to him.

What we have just said is attested by experience so conspicuously, that it is in the mouth of nearly everyone: "Man is to man a God." Yet *it rarely happens that men live in obedience to reason, for things are so ordered among them that they are generally envious and troublesome one to another.* Nevertheless they are scarcely able to lead a solitary life, so that the definition of man as a social animal has met with general assent; in fact, men do derive from social life much more convenience than injury. Let satirists then laugh their fill at human affairs, let theologians rail, and let misanthropes praise to their utmost the life of untutored rusticity, let them heap contempt on men and praises on beasts; when all is said, they will find that men can provide for their wants much more easily by mutual help, and that only by uniting their forces can they escape from the dangers that on every side beset them: not to say how much more excellent and worthy of our knowledge it is, to study the actions of men than the actions of beasts.

The highest good of those who follow virtue is common to all, and therefore all can equally rejoice therein.

Someone may ask how it would be, if the highest good of those who follow after virtue were not common to all? Would it not then follow, as above, that men living in obedience to reason, that is, men insofar as they agree in nature, would be at variance one with another? To such an inquiry I make answer, that it follows not accidentally but from the very nature of reason, that man's highest good is common to all, inasmuch as it is deduced from the very essence of man, insofar as defined by reason; and that a man could neither be, nor be conceived without the power of taking pleasure in this highest good. For it belongs to the essence of the human mind to have an adequate knowledge of the eternal and infinite essence of God.

The good which every man who follows after virtue desires for himself he will also desire for other men, and so much the more, in proportion as he has a greater knowledge of God.

He who, guided by emotion only, endeavors to cause others to love what he loves himself, and to make the rest of the world live according to his own fancy, acts solely by impulse, and is, therefore, hateful, especially to those who take delight in something different, and accordingly study and, by similar impulse, endeavor to make men live in accordance with what pleases themselves.

Again, as the highest good sought by men under the guidance of emotion is often such that it can only be possessed by a single individual, it follows that those who love it are not consistent in their intentions, but, while they delight to sing its praises, fear to be believed. But he who endeavors to lead men by reason, does not act by impulse but courteously and kindly, and his intention is always consistent.

Again, whatsoever we desire and do, whereof we are the cause insofar as we possess the idea of God, or know God, I set down to Religion. The desire of well-doing, which is engendered by a life according to reason, I call *piety*. Further, the desire whereby a man living according to reason is bound to associate others with himself in friendship, I call *honor;* by *honorable* I mean that which is praised by men living according to reason, and by *base* I mean that which is repugnant to the gaining of friendship.

I have also shown in addition what are the foundations of a state; and the difference between true virtue and infirmity may be readily gathered from what I have said; namely, that true virtue is nothing else but living in accordance with reason; while infirmity is nothing else but man's allowing himself to be led by things which are external to himself, and to be by them determined to act in a manner demanded by the general disposition of things rather than by his own nature considered solely in itself.

The rational quest of what is useful to us further teaches us the necessity of associating ourselves with our fellowmen, but not with beasts, or things, whose nature is different from our own; we have the same rights in respect to them as they have in respect to us.

Nay, as everyone's right is defined by his virtue, or power, men have far greater rights over beasts than beasts have over men. Still I do not deny that beasts feel: what I deny is that we may not consult our own advantage and use them as we please, treating them in the way which best suits us; for their nature is not like ours, and their emotions are naturally different from human emotions.

Every man exists by sovereign natural right, and, consequently, by sovereign natural right performs those actions which follow from the necessity of his own nature; therefore by sovereign natural right every man judges what is good and what is bad, takes care of his own advantage according to his own disposition, avenges the wrongs done to him, and endeavors to preserve that which he loves and to destroy that which he hates. Now, if men lived under the guidance of reason, everyone would remain in possession of this his right, without any injury being done to his neighbor. But seeing that they are a prey to their emotions, which far surpass human power or virtue, they are often drawn in different directions, and being at variance one with another, stand in need of mutual help. Wherefore, in order that men may live together in harmony, and may aid one another, it is necessary that they should forego their natural right, and, for the sake of security, refrain from all actions which can injure their fellowmen. An emotion can only be restrained by an emotion stronger than, and contrary to itself, and men avoid inflicting injury through fear of incurring a greater injury themselves.

On this law society can be established, so long as it keeps in its own hand the right, possessed by everyone, of avenging injury, and pronouncing on good and evil; and provided it also possesses the power to lay down a general rule of conduct, and to pass laws sanctioned, not by reason, which is powerless in restraining emotion, but by threats.

Such a society established with laws and the power of preserving itself is called a State, while those who live under its protection are called citizens. We may readily understand that there is in the state of nature nothing which by universal consent is pronounced good or bad; for in the state of nature everyone thinks solely of his own advantage, and according to his disposition, with reference only to his individual advantage, decides what is good or bad, being bound by no law to anyone besides himself.

In the state of nature, therefore, sin is inconceivable; it can only exist in a State, where good and evil are pronounced on by common consent, and where everyone is bound to obey the State authority. Sin, then, is nothing else but disobedience, which is therefore punished by the right of the State only. Obedience, on the other hand, is set down as merit, inasmuch as a man is thought worthy of merit, if he takes delight in the advantages which a State provides.

Again, in the state of nature, no one is by common consent master of anything, nor is there anything in nature which can be said to belong to one man rather than another: *all things are common to all.* Hence, in the state of nature, we can conceive no wish to render to every man his own, or to deprive a man of that which belongs to him; in other words, there is nothing in the state of nature answering to justice and injustice. Such ideas are only possible in a social state, when it is decreed by common consent what belongs to one man and what to another.

From all these considerations it is evident that justice and injustice, sin and merit, are extrinsic ideas, and not attributes which display the nature of the mind.

Whatsoever disposes the human body, so as to render it capable of being affected in an increased number of ways, or of affecting external bodies in an increased number of ways, is useful to man; and is so, in proportion as the body is thereby rendered more capable of being affected or affecting other bodies in an increased number of ways; contrariwise, whatsoever renders the body less capable in this respect is hurtful to man.

Whatsoever brings about the preservation of the proportion of motion and rest, which parts of the human body mutually possess, is good; contrariwise, whatsoever causes a change in such proportion is bad.

I would here remark that I consider that a body undergoes death, when the proportion of motion and rest which obtained mutually among its several parts is changed. For I do not venture to deny that a human body, while keeping the circulation of the blood and other properties, wherein the life of a body is thought to consist, may nonetheless be changed into another nature totally different from its own. There is no reason which compels me to maintain that body does not die unless it becomes a corpse; nay, experience would seem to point to the opposite conclusion. *It sometimes happens, that a man undergoes such changes, that I should hardly call him the same.*

I have heard tell of a certain Spanish poet, who had been seized with sickness, and though he recovered therefrom yet remained so oblivious of his past life that he would not believe the plays and tragedies he had written to be his own: indeed, he might have been taken for a grown-up child, if he had also forgotten his native tongue. If this instance seems incredible, what shall we say of infants? A man of ripe age deems their nature so unlike his own, that he can only be persuaded that he too has been an infant by the analogy of other men. However, I prefer to leave such questions undiscussed, lest I should give ground to the superstitious for raising new issues.

Whatsoever conduces to man's social life, or causes men to live together in harmony, is useful, whereas whatsoever brings discord into a State is bad.

Pleasure in itself is not bad but good: contrariwise, pain in itself is bad.

Mirth cannot be excessive, but is always good; contrariwise, melancholy is always bad.

Stimulation may be excessive and bad; on the other hand, grief may be good, insofar as stimulation or pleasure is bad.

Love and desire may be excessive.

Mirth is pleasure which, insofar as it is referred to the body, consists in all parts of the body being affected equally. That is, the body's power of activity is increased or aided in such a manner that the several parts maintain their former proportion of rest and motion.

Mirth, which I have stated to be good, can be conceived more easily than it can be observed. For the emotions, whereby we are daily assailed, are generally referred to some part of the body which is affected more than the rest; hence the emotions are generally excessive, and so fix the mind in the contemplation of one object that it is unable to think of others; and although men, as a rule, are a prey to many emotions—and very few are found who are always assailed by one and the same—yet there are cases where one and the same emotion remains obstinately fixed.

We sometimes see men so absorbed in one object that, although it be not present, they think they have it before them; when this is the case with a man who is not asleep, we say he is delirious or mad; nor are those persons who are inflamed with love, and who dream all night and all day about nothing but their mistress, or some woman, considered as less mad, for they are made objects of ridicule.

But when a miser thinks of nothing but gain or money, or when an ambitions man thinks of nothing but glory, they are not reckoned to be mad, because they are generally harmful, and are thought worthy of being hated. But, in reality, avarice, ambition, lust, etc., are species of madness, though they may not be reckoned among diseases.

Hatred can never be good.

Here, and in what follows, I mean by hatred only hatred toward men.

Envy, derision, contempt, anger, revenge, and other emotions attributable to hatred, or arising therefrom, are bad.

Whatsoever we desire from motives of hatred is base, and in a State unjust.

The Little Pleasures
and the Great Sin

Between derision and laughter I recognize a great difference. For laughter, as also jocularity, is merely pleasure; therefore, so long as it be not excessive, it is in itself good. Assuredly nothing forbids man to enjoy himself, save grim and gloomy superstition. For why is it more lawful to satiate one's hunger and thirst than to drive away one's melancholy? I reason, and have convinced myself as follows: No deity, nor anyone else, save the envious, takes pleasure in my infirmity and discomfort, nor sets down to my virtue the tears, sobs, fear, and the like, which are signs of infirmity of spirit; on the contrary, the greater the pleasure wherewith we are affected, the greater the perfection whereto we pass; in other words, the more must we necessarily partake of the divine nature.

Therefore, to make use of what comes in our way, and to enjoy it as much as possible (not to the point of satiety for that would not be enjoyment) is the part of a wise man. I say *it is the part of a wise man to refresh and recreate himself with moderate and pleasant food and drink, and also with perfumes, with the soft beauty of growing plants, with dress, with music, with many sports, with theatres, and the like, such as every man may make use of without injury to his neighbor.*

For the human body is composed of very numerous parts, of diverse nature, which continually stand in need of fresh and varied nourishment, so that the whole body may be equally capable of performing all the actions which follow from the necessity of its own nature; and, consequently, so that the mind may also be equally capable of understanding many things simultaneously. This way of life, then, agrees best with our principles, and also with general practice; therefore, if there be any question of another plan the plan we have mentioned is the best and in every way to be commended.

He who lives under the guidance of reason endeavors, as far as possible, to render back love, or kindness, for other men's hatred, anger, contempt, etc., toward him.

He who chooses to avenge wrongs with hatred is assuredly wretched. But he who strives to conquer hatred with love, fights his battle in joy and confidence; he withstands many as easily as one, and has very little need of fortune's aid. Those whom he vanquishes yield joyfully, not through failure, but through increase in their powers; all these conse-

108

quences follow so plainly from the mere definitions of love and understanding, that I have no need to prove them in detail.

Emotions of hope and fear cannot be in themselves good.

We may add that these emotions show defective knowledge and an absence of power in the mind; for the same reason confidence, despair, joy, and disappointment are signs of a want of mental power. For although confidence and joy are pleasurable emotions, they nevertheless imply a preceding pain, namely, hope and fear. Wherefore the more we endeavor to be guided by reason, the less do we depend on hope; we endeavor to free ourselves from fear, and, as far as we can, to dominate fortune, directing our actions by the sure counsels of wisdom.

The emotions of overesteem and disparagement are always bad.

Overesteem is apt to render its object proud.

Pity, in a man who lives under the guidance of reason, is in itself bad and useless.

He who rightly realizes that all things follow from the necessity of the divine nature, and come to pass in accordance with the eternal laws and rules of nature, will not find anything worthy of hatred, derision, or contempt, nor will he bestow pity on anything, but to the utmost extent of human virtue he will endeavor to do well, as the saying is, and to rejoice.

We may add that he who is easily touched with compassion, and is moved by another's sorrow or tears, often does something which he afterwards regrets; partly because we can never be sure that an action caused by emotion is good, partly because we are easily deceived by false tears. I am in this place expressly speaking of a man living under the guidance of reason.

He who is moved to help others neither by reason nor by compassion, is rightly styled inhuman, for he seems unlike a man.

Approval is not repugnant to reason. but can agree therewith and arise therefrom.

He who lives under the guidance of reason, desires for others the good which he seeks for himself; wherefore from seeing someone doing good to his fellow his own endeavor to do good is aided; in other words, he will feel pleasure accompanied by the idea of the benefactor. Therefore he approves of him.

Indignation as we defined it is necessarily evil; we may, however, remark that when the sovereign power for the sake of preserving peace punishes a citizen who has injured another, it should not be said to be indignant with the criminal, for it is not incited by hatred to ruin him; it is led by a sense of duty to punish him.

Self-approval may arise from reason, and that which arises from reason is the highest possible.

Self-approval is in reality the highest object for which we can hope. For no one endeavors to preserve his being for the sake of any ulterior object, and, as this approval is more and more fostered and strengthened by praise, and on the contrary is more and more disturbed by blame, fame becomes the most powerful of incitements to action, and life under disgrace is almost unendurable.

Humility is not a virtue, or does not arise from reason.

Repentance is not a virtue, or does not arise from reason; but he who repents of an action is doubly wretched or infirm.

As men seldom live under the guidance of reason, these two emotions, namely, humility and repentance, as also hope and fear, bring more good than harm; hence, as we must sin, we had better sin in that direction. For, if all men who are a prey to emotion were all equally proud, they would shrink from nothing, and would fear nothing; how then could they be joined and linked together in bonds of union?

The crowd plays the tyrant, when it is not in fear; hence we need not wonder that the prophets, who consulted the good, not of a few, but of all, so strenuously commended humility, repentance, and reverence. Indeed those who are a prey to these emotions may be led much more easily than others to live under the guidance of reason, that is, to become free and to enjoy the life of the blessed.

Extreme pride or dejection indicates extreme ignorance of self.

Extreme pride or dejection indicates extreme infirmity of spirit.

Hence it most clearly follows, that the proud and the dejected specially fall a prey to the emotions.

Yet dejection can be more easily corrected than pride; for the latter being a pleasurable emotion, and the former a painful emotion, the pleasurable is stronger than the painful.

The proud man delights in the company of flatterers and parasites, but hates the company of the highminded.

Pride
and Dejection

It would be too long a task to enumerate here all the evil results of pride, inasmuch as the proud are a prey to all the emotions, though to none of them less than to love and pity. I cannot, however, pass over in silence the fact that a man may be called proud from his underestimation of other people; and, therefore, pride in this sense may be defined as pleasure arising from the false opinion whereby a man may consider himself superior to his fellows.

The dejection, which is the opposite quality to this sort of pride, may be defined as pain arising from the false opinion whereby a man may think himself inferior to his fellows. Such being the case, we can easily see that a proud man is necessarily envious and only takes pleasure in the company who fool his weak mind to the top of his bent, and make him insane instead of merely foolish.

Though dejection is the emotion contrary to pride, yet is the dejected man very near akin to the proud man. For, inasmuch as his pain arises from a comparison between his own infirmity and other men's power or virtue, it will be removed, or, in other words, he will feel pleasure, if his imagination be occupied in contemplating other men's faults; whence arises the proverb, "The unhappy are comforted by finding fellow-sufferers." Contrariwise, he will be more pained in proportion as he thinks himself inferior to others; hence none are so prone to envy as the dejected, they are specially keen in observing men's actions with a view to fault-finding rather than correction, in order to reserve their praises for dejection, and to glory therein, though all the time with a dejected air. These effects follow as necessarily from the said emotion, as it follows from the nature of a triangle that the three angles are equal to two right angles

I have already said that I call these and similar emotions bad, solely in respect to what is useful to man. The laws of nature have regard to nature's general order, whereof man is but a part. I mention this in passing lest any should think that I have wished to set forth the faults and irrational deeds of men rather than the nature and properties of things. For *I regard human emotions and their properties as on the same footing with other natural phenomena.* Assuredly human emotions indicate the power and ingenuity of nature, if not of human nature, quite as fully as other things which we admire, and which we delight to contemplate.

Honor is not repugnant to reason, but may arise therefrom.

Empty honor, as it is styled, is self-approval, fostered only by the good opinion of the populace; when this good opinion ceases there ceases also the self-approval, in other words, the highest object of each man's love; consequently, he whose honor is rooted in popular approval must, day by day, anxiously strive, act, and scheme in order to retain his reputation. For the populace is variable and inconstant, so that, if a reputation be not kept up, it quickly withers away.

Everyone wishes to catch popular applause for himself, and readily represses the fame of others. The object of the strife being estimated as the greatest of all goods, each combatant is seized with a fierce desire to put down his rivals in every possible way, till he who at last comes out victorious is more proud of having done harm to others than of having done good to himself. This sort of honor, then, is really empty, being nothing.

The points to note concerning shame may easily be inferred from what was said on the subject of mercy and repentance. I will only add that shame, like compassion, though not a virtue, is yet good, insofar as it shows that the feeler of shame is really imbued with the desire to live honorably; in the same way as suffering is good, as showing that the injured part is not mortified. Therefore, though a man who feels shame is sorrowful, he is yet more perfect than he who is shameless, and has no desire to live honorably.

To all the actions whereto we are determined by emotion wherein the mind is passive, we can be determined without emotion by reason.

A given action is called bad, insofar as it arises from one being affected by hatred or any evil emotion. But no action, considered in itself alone, is either good or bad, one and the same action being sometimes good, sometimes bad; wherefore to the action which is sometimes bad, or arises from some evil emotion, we may be led by reason.

An example will put this point in a clearer light. The action of striking, insofar is it is considered physically, and insofar as we merely look to the fact that a man raises his arm, clenches his fist, and moves his whole arm violently downward, is a virtue or excellence which is conceived as proper to the structure of the human body.

If, then, a man, moved by anger or hatred, is led to clench his fist or to move his arm, this result takes place, because one and the same action can be associated with various mental images of things; therefore we may be determined to the performance of one and the same action by confused ideas, or by clear and distinct ideas. Hence it is evident that every desire which springs from emotion, wherein the mind is passive, would become useless if men could be guided by reason. Let us now see why desire which arises from emotion, wherein the mind is passive, is called by us blind.

Desire arising from a pleasure or pain that is not attributable to the whole body, but only to one or certain parts thereof, is without utility in respect to a man as a whole.

As pleasure is generally attributed to one part of the body, we generally desire to preserve our being without taking into consideration our health as a whole: to which it may be added that the desires which have most hold over us take account of the present and not of the future.

Desire which springs from reason cannot be excessive.

Insofar as the mind conceives a thing under the dictates of reason, it is affected equally, whether the idea be of a thing future, past, or present.

If we could possess an adequate knowledge of the duration of things, and could determine by reason their periods of existence, we should contemplate things future with the same emotion as things present; and the mind would desire as though it were present the good which it conceived as future; consequently it would necessarily neglect a lesser good in the present for the sake of a greater good in the future, and would in no wise desire that which is good in the present but a source of evil in the future, as we shall presently show.

However, we can have but a very inadequate knowledge of the duration of things; and the periods of their existence we can only determine by imagination, which is not so powerfully affected by the future as by the present. Hence such true knowledge of good and evil as we possess is merely abstract or general, and the judgement which we pass on the order of things and the connection of causes, with a view to determining what is good or bad for us in the present, is rather imaginary than real.

Therefore it is nothing wonderful if the desire arising from such knowledge of good and evil, insofar as it looks on into the future, be more readily checked than the desire of things which are agreeable at the present time.

He who is led by fear, and does good in order to escape evil, is not led by reason.

Superstitious persons, who know better how to rail at vice than how to teach virtue, and who strive not to guide men by reason, but so to restrain them that they would rather escape evil than love virtue, have no other aim but to make others as wretched as themselves; wherefore it is nothing wonderful if they be generally troublesome and odious to their fellow men.

Under desire which springs from reason, we seek good directly, and shun evil indirectly.

This may be illustrated by the example of a sick and a healthy man. The sick man through fear of death eats what he naturally shrinks from, but the healthy man takes pleasure in his food, and thus gets a better enjoyment out of life than if he were in fear of death, and desired directly to avoid it. So a judge, who condemns a criminal to death, not from hatred or anger but from love of the public well-being, is guided solely by reason.

The idea of evil is an inadequate knowledge.

Hence it follows that, if the human mind possessed only adequate ideas, it would form no conception of evil.

Under the guidance of reason we should pursue the greater of two goods and the lesser of two evils.

We may, under the guidance of reason, pursue the lesser evil as though it were the greater good, and we may shun the lesser good, which would be the cause of the greater evil. For the evil, which is here called the lesser, is really good, and the lesser good is really evil, wherefore we may seek the former and shun the latter.

We may, under the guidance of reason, seek a greater good in the future in preference to a lesser good in the present, and we may seek a lesser evil in the present in preference to a greater evil in the future.

We may, under the guidance of reason, seek a lesser evil in the present, because it is the cause of a greater good in the future, and we may shun a lesser good in the present, because it is the cause of a greater evil in the future.

The Free Man

A free man thinks of death least of all things; and his wisdom is a meditation not of death but of life.

If men were born free, they would, so long as they remained free, form no conception of good and evil.

The virtue of a free man is seen to be as great when it declines dangers, as when it overcomes them.

The free man is as courageous in timely retreat as in combat; or, a free man shows equal courage or presence of mind, whether he elect to give battle or to retreat.

The free man who lives among the ignorant, strives, as far as he can, to avoid receiving favors from them.

I say, as far as he can. For though men be ignorant, yet are they men, and in cases of necessity could afford us human aid, the most excellent of all things: therefore it is often necessary to accept favors from them, and consequently to repay such favors in kind; we must, therfore, exercise caution in declining favors, lest we should have the appearance of despising those who bestow them, or of being, from avaricious motives, unwilling to requite them, and so give ground for offense by the very fact of striving to avoid it. Thus, in declining favors, we must look to the requirements of utility and courtesy.

Only free men are thoroughly grateful one to another.

The good-will which men who are led by blind desire have for one another, is generally a bargaining or enticement, rather than pure good-will. Moreover, ingratitude is not an emotion. Yet it is base, inasmuch as it generally shows that a man is affected by excessive hatred, anger, pride, avarice, etc.

He who, by reason of his folly, knows not how to return benefits, is not ungrateful, much less he who is not won over by the gifts of a courtesan to serve her lust, or by a thief to conceal his thefts, or by any similar persons. Contrariwise, such a one shows a constant mind, inasmuch as he cannot by any gifts be corrupted, to his own or the general hurt.

The free man never acts fraudulently, but always in good faith.

The man who is guided by reason, is more free in a State, where he lives under a general system of law, than in solitude, where he is independent.

These and similar observations which we have made on man's true freedom, may be referred to strength, that is, to courage and nobility of character. I do not think it worth while to prove separately all the properties of strength; much less need I show that he that is strong hates no man, is angry with no man, envies no man, is indignant with no man, despises no man, and least of all things is proud. The strong man has ever first in his thoughts that all things follow from the necessity of the divine nature; so that whatsoever he deems to be hurtful and evil, and whatsoever, accordingly, seems to him impious, horrible, unjust, and base assumes that appearance owing to his own disordered fragmentary, and confused view of the universe.

Wherefore he strives before all things to conceive things as they really are, and to remove the hindrances to true knowledge, such as are hatred, anger, envy, derision, pride, and similar emotions, which I have mentioned above. Thus he endeavors, as we said before, as far as in him lies, to do good, and to go on his way rejoicing.

All our endeavors or desires so follow from the necessity of our nature, that they can be understood either through it alone, as their proximate cause, or by virtue of our being a part of nature, which cannot be adequately conceived through itself without other individuals.

Desires which follow from our nature in such a manner that they can be understood through it alone, are those which are referred to the mind, insofar as the latter is conceived to consist of adequate ideas: the remaining desires are only referred to the mind insofar as it conceives things inadequately, and their force and increase are generally defined not by the power of man, but by the power of things external to us: wherefore the former are rightly called actions, the latter passions, for the former always indicate our power, the latter, on the other hand, show our infirmity and fragmentary knowledge.

Our actions, that is, those desires which are defined by man's power or reason, are always good. The rest may be either good or bad.

Thus in life it is before all things useful to perfect the understanding, or reason, as far as we can, and in this alone man's highest happiness or blessedness consists, indeed blessedness is nothing else but the contentment of spirit which arises from the intuitive knowledge of God: now, to perfect the understanding is nothing else but to understand God, God's attributes, and the actions which follow from the necessity of his nature. Wherefore of a man who is led by reason, the ultimate aim or highest desire, whereby he seeks to govern all his fellows, is that whereby he is brought to the adequate conception of himself and of all things within the scope of his intelligence.

Therefore, without intelligence there is not rational life: and things are only good insofar as they aid man in his enjoyment of the intellectual life, which is defined by intelligence. Contrariwise, *whatsoever things hinder man's perfecting of his reason, and capability to enjoy the rational life, are alone called evil.*

As all things whereof man is the efficient cause are necessarily good, no evil can befall man except through external causes; namely, by virtue of man being a part of universal nature, whose laws human nature is compelled to obey, and to conform to in almost infinite ways.

It is impossible that man should not be a part of nature, or that he should not follow her general order, but if he be thrown among individuals whose nature is in harmony with his own, his power of action will thereby be aided and fostered, whereas, if he be thrown among such as are but very little in harmony with his nature, he will hardly be able to accommodate himself to them without undergoing a great change himself.

Whatsoever in nature we deem to be evil, or to be capable of injuring our faculty for existing and enjoying the rational life, we may endeavor to remove in whatever way seems safest to us; on the other hand, whatsoever we deem to be good or useful for preserving our being, and enabling us to enjoy the rational life, we may appropriate to our use and employ as we think best. Everyone without exception may, by sovereign right of nature, do whatsoever he thinks will advance his own interest.

Nothing can be in more harmony with the nature of any given thing than other individuals of the same species; therefore for man in the preservation of his being and the enjoyment of the rational life there is nothing more useful than his fellow man who is led by reason. Further, as we know not anything among individual things which is more excellent than a man led by reason, no man can better display the power of his skill and disposition than in so training men that they come at last to live under the dominion of their own reason.

Insofar as men are influenced by envy or any kind of hatred, one toward another, they are at variance, and are therefore to be feared in proportion as they are more powerful than their fellows.

Yet *minds are not conquered by force, but by love and highmindedness.*

It is before all things useful to men to associate their ways of life, to bind themselves together with such bonds as they think most fitted to gather them all into unity, and generally to do whatsoever serves to strengthen friendship.

But for this there is need of skill and watchfulness. For men are diverse (seeing that those who live under the guidance of reason are few), yet are they generally envious and more prone to revenge than to sympathy. No small force of character is therefore required to take everyone as he is, and to restrain one's self from imitating the emotions of others. But those who carp at mankind, and are more skilled in railing at vice than in instilling virtue, and who break rather than strengthen men's dispositions, are hurtful both to themselves and others. Thus many from too great impatience of spirit, or from misguided religious zeal, have preferred to live among brutes rather than among men; as boys or youths, who cannot peaceably endure the chidings of their parents, will enlist as soldiers and choose the hardships of war and the despotic discipline in preference to the comforts of home and the admonitions of their father: suffering any burden to be put upon them, so long as they may spite their parents.

Therefore, although men are generally governed in everything by their own lusts, yet their association in common brings many more advantages than drawbacks. Wherefore it is better to bear patiently the wrongs they may do us, and to strive to promote whatsoever serves to bring about harmony and friendship.

Those things which beget harmony are such as are attributable to justice, equity, and honorable living. For men brook ill not only what is unjust or iniquitous, but also what is reckoned disgraceful, or that a man should slight the received customs of their society. For winning love those qualities are especially necessary which have regard to religion and piety.

Further, harmony is often the result of fear: but such harmony is insecure. Further, fear arises from infirmity of spirit, and moreover belongs not to the exercise of reason: the same is true of compassion, though this latter seems to bear a certain resemblance to piety.

Men are also gained over by liberality, especially such as have not the means to buy what is necessary to sustain life, However, to give aid to every man is far beyond the power and the advantage of any private person. For the riches of any private person are wholly inadequate to meet such a call. Again, *an individual man's resources of character are too limited for him to be able to make all men his friends.* Hence providing for the poor is a duty which falls on the State as a whole, and has regard only to the general advantage.

In accepting favors, and in returning gratitude our duty must be wholly different.

Again, meretricious love, that is, the lust of generation arising from bodily beauty, and generally every sort of love which owns anything save freedom of soul as its cause, readily passes into hate; unless indeed, what is worse, it is a species of madness; and then it promotes discord rather than harmony.

As concerning marriage, it is certain that this is in harmony with reason, if the desire for physical union be not engendered solely by bodily beauty, but also by the desire to beget children and to train them up wisely; and moreover, if the love of both, to wit, of the man and of the woman, is not caused by bodily beauty only, but also by freedom of soul.

Furthermore, flattery begets harmony; but only by means of the vile offense of slavishness or treachery. None are more readily taken with flattery than the proud, who wish to be first, but are not.

There is in abasement a spurious appearance of piety and religion. Although abasement is the opposite to pride, yet is he that abases himself akin to the proud.

Shame also brings about harmony, but only in such matter as cannot be hid. Further, as shame is a species of pain, it does not concern the exercise of reason.

The remaining emotions of pain toward men are directly opposed to justice, equity, honor, piety, and religion; and, although indignation seems to bear a certain resemblance to equity, yet is life but lawless where every man may pass judgment on another's deeds, and vindicate his own or other men's rights.

Correctness of conduct, that is, the desire of pleasing men which is determined by reason, is attributable to piety. But, if it spring from emotion, it is ambition, or the desire whereby men, under the false cloak of piety, generally stir up discords and seditions.

For he who desires to aid his fellows either in word or in deed, so that they may together enjoy the highest good, he, I say will before all things strive to win them over with love: not to draw them into admiration, so that a system may be called after his name, nor to give any cause for envy. Further, in his conversation he will shrink from talking of men's faults, and will be careful to speak but sparingly of human infirmity: but he will dwell at length on human virtue or power, and the way whereby it may be perfected. Thus will men be stirred not by fear, nor by aversion, but only by the emotion of joy, to endeavor, so far as in them lies, to live in obedience to reason.

Besides men, we know of no particular thing in nature in whose mind we may rejoice, and whom we can associate with ourselves in friendship or any sort of fellowship; therefore, whatsoever there be in nature besides man, a regard for our advantage does not call on us to preserve, but to preserve or destroy according to its various capabilities, and to adapt to our use as best we may.

The advantage which we derive from things external to us, besides the experience and knowledge which we acquire from observing them, and from recombining their elements in different forms, is principally the preservation of the body; from this point of view, those things are most useful which can so feed and nourish the body that all its parts may rightly fulfill their functions.

For, in proportion as the body is capable of being affected in a greater variety of ways, and of affecting external bodies in a great number of ways, so much the more is the mind capable of thinking. But there seem to be very few things of this kind in nature; wherefore for the due nourishment of the body we must use many foods of diverse nature.

For the human body is composed of very many parts of different nature, which stand in continual need of varied nourishment, so that the whole body may be equally capable of doing everything that can follow from its own nature, and consequently that the mind also may be equally capable of forming many perceptions.

Now for providing these nourishments the strength of each individual would hardly suffice, if men did not lend one another mutual aid. But money has furnished us with a token for everything: hence it is with the notion of money that the mind of the multitude is chiefly engrossed: nay, it can hardly conceive any kind of pleasure which is not accompanied with the idea of money as cause.

This result is the fault only of those who seek money, not from poverty or to supply their necessary wants, but because they have learned the arts of gain, wherewith they bring themselves to great splendor. Certainly they nourish their bodies, according to custom, but scantily, believing that they lose as much of their wealth as they spend on the preservation of their body. But they who know the true use of money, and who fix the measure of wealth solely with regard to their actual needs, live content with little.

As, therefore, those things are good which assist the various parts of the body, and enable them to perform their functions; and as pleasure consists in an increase of, or aid to, man's power, insofar as he is composed of mind and body; it follows that all those things which bring pleasure are good.

But seeing that things do not work with the object of giving us pleasure, and that their power of action is not tempered to suit our advantage, and, lastly, that pleasure is generally referred to one part of the body more than to the other parts; therefore most emotions of pleasure (unless reason and watchfulness be at hand), and consequently the desires arising therefrom, may become excessive. Moreover we may add that emotion leads us to pay most regard to what is agreeable in the present, nor can we estimate what is future with emotions equally vivid.

Superstition, on the other hand, seems to account as good all that brings pain, and as bad all that brings pleasure. However, as we said above, none but the envious take delight in my infirmity and trouble.

For the greater the pleasure whereby we are affected, the greater is the perfection whereto we pass, and consequently the more do we partake of the divine nature: no pleasure can ever be evil, which is regulated by a true regard for our advantage. But contrariwise he who is led by fear and does good only to avoid evil, is not guided by reason.

But human power is extremely limited, and is infinitely surpassed by the power of external causes; we have not, therefore, an absolute power of shaping to our use those things which are without us.

Nevertheless, we shall bear with an equal mind all that happens to us in contravention to the claims of our own advantage, so long as we are conscious that we have done our duty, and that the power which we possess is not sufficient to enable us to protect ourselves completely; remembering that we are a part of universal nature, and that we follow her order. If we have a clear and distinct understanding of this, that part of our nature which is defined by intelligence, in other words the better part of ourselves, will assuredly acquiesce in what befalls us, and in such acquiescence will endeavor to persist.

For, insofar as we are intelligent beings, we cannot desire anything save that which is necessary, nor yield absolute acquiescence to anything save to that which is true: wherefore, insofar as we have a right understanding of these things, the endeavor of the better part of ourselves is in harmony with the order of nature as a whole.

On the Power of the Intellect

or,

The Freedom of Man

Even as thoughts and the ideas of things are arranged and associated in the mind, so are the modifications of body on the images of things precisely in the same way arranged and associated in the body.

If we remove a disturbance of the spirit, or emotion, from the thought of an external cause, and unite it to other thoughts, then will the love or hatred toward that external cause, and also the vacillations of spirit which arise from these emotions, be destroyed.

An emotion which is a passion ceases to be a passion as soon as we form a clear and distinct idea thereof.

An emotion comes more under our control, and the mind is less passive in respect to it, in proportion as it is more known to us.

There is no modification of the body whereof we cannot form some clear and distinct conception.

Hence it follows that there is no emotion whereof we cannot form some clear and distinct conception.

For an emotion is the idea of a modification of the body, and must therefore involve some clear and distinct conception.

Seeing that there is nothing which is not followed by an effect, and that we clearly and distinctly understand whatever follows from an idea which in us is adequate, it follows that everyone has the power of clearly and distinctly understanding himself and his emotions, if not absolutely, at any rate in part, and consequently of bringing it about that he should become less subject to them.

To attain this result, therefore, we must chiefly direct our efforts to acquiring, as far as possible, a clear and distinct knowledge of every emotion, in order that the mind may thus, through emotion, be determined to think of those things which it clearly and distinctly perceives, and wherein it fully acquiesces: and thus that the emotion itself may be separated from the thought of an external cause, and may be associated with true thoughts; whence it will come to pass, not only that love, hatred, etc. will be destroyed, but also that the appetites or desires which are wont to arise from such emotion, will become incapable of being excessive. For it must be especially remarked that the appetite through which a man is said to be active, and that through which he is said to be passive, is one and the same.

For instance, we have shown that human nature is so constituted, that everyone desires his fellow men to live after his own fashion; in a man who is not guided by reason, this appetite is a passion which is called ambition, and does not greatly differ from pride; whereas in a man who lives by the dictates of reason, it is an activity or virtue which is called piety.

In like manner all appetites or desires are only passions, insofar as they spring from inadequate ideas; the same results are accredited to virtue, when they are aroused or generated by adequate ideas. For all desires, whereby we are determined to any given action, may arise as much from adequate as from inadequate ideas. Than this remedy for the emotions, which consists in a true knowledge thereof, nothing more excellent, being within our power, can be devised. For the mind has no other power save that of thinking and of forming adequate ideas, as we have shown above.

To conceive a thing as free can be nothing else than to conceive it simply, while we are in ignorance of the cause whereby it has been determined to action.

An emotion toward a thing which we conceive simply, and not as necessary, or as contingent, or as possible, is, other conditions being equal, greater than any other emotion.

The mind has greater power over the emotions and is less subject thereto, insofar as it understands all things as necessary.

The more this knowledge, that things are necessary, is applied to particular things, which we conceive more distinctly and vividly, the greater is the power of the mind over the emotions, as experience also testifies. For we see that the pain arising from the loss of any good is mitigated as soon as the man who has lost it perceives that it could not by any means have been preserved.

So also we see that no one pities an infant because it cannot speak, walk, or reason, or lastly, because it passes so many years, as it were, in unconsciousness. Whereas, if most people were born full-blown and only one here and there as an infant, everyone would pity the infants; because infancy would not then be looked on as a state natural and necessary, but as a fault or delinquency in Nature; and we may note several other instances of the same sort.

Emotions which are aroused or spring from reason, if we take account of time, are stronger than those which are attributable to particular objects that we regard as absent.

An emotion is stronger in proportion to the number of simultaneous concurrent causes whereby it is aroused.

An emotion which is attributable to many and diverse causes which the mind regards as simultaneous with the emotion itself, is less hurtful, and we are less subject thereto and less affected toward each of its causes, than if it were a different and equally powerful emotion attributable to fewer causes or to a single cause.

So long as we are not assailed by emotions contrary to our nature, we have the power of arranging and associating the modifications of our body according to the intellectual order.

By this power of rightly arranging and associating the bodily modifications we can guard ourselves from being easily affected by evil emotions.

The best we can do, therefore, so long as we do not possess a perfect knowledge of our emotions, is to frame a system of right conduct, or fixed practical precepts, to commit it to memory, and to apply it constantly to the particular circumstances which now and again meet us in life, so that our imagination may become fully imbued therewith, and that it may be always ready to our hand.

For instance, we have laid down among the rules of life that hatred should be overcome with love or highmindedness, and not requited with hatred in return. Now, that this precept of reason may be always ready to our hand in time of need, we should often think over and reflect upon the wrongs generally committed by men, and in what manner and way they may be best warded off by highmindedness: we shall thus associate the idea of wrong with the idea of this precept, which accordingly will always be ready for use when a wrong is done to us.

If we keep also in readiness the notion of our true advantage, and of the good which follows from mutual friendships, and common fellowships; further, if we remember that complete acquiescence is the result of the right way of life, and that men, no less than everything else, act by the necessity of their nature: in such case I say the wrong, or the hatred which commonly arises therefrom, will engross a very small part of our imagination and will be easily overcome; or, if the anger which springs from a grievous wrong be not overcome easily, it will nevertheless be overcome, though not without a spiritual conflict, far sooner than if we had not thus reflected on the subject beforehand.

We should, in the same way, reflect on courage as a means of overcoming fear; the ordinary dangers of life should frequently be brought to mind and imagined, together with the means whereby through readiness of resource and strength of mind we can avoid and overcome them. But we must note that in arranging our thoughts and conceptions we should always bear in mind that which is good in every individual thing, in order that we may always be determined to action by an emotion of pleasure.

For instance, if a man sees that he is too keen in the pursuit of honor, let him think over its right use, the end for which it should be pursued, and the means whereby he may attain it. Let him not think of its misuse, and its emptiness, and the fickleness of mankind, and the like, whereof no man thinks except through a morbidness of disposition; with thoughts like these do the most ambitious most torment themselves, when they despair of gaining the distinctions they hanker after, and in thus giving vent to their anger would fain appear wise. Wherefore it is certain that those who cry out the loudest against the misuse of honor and the vanity of the world, are those who most greedily covet it.

This is not peculiar to the ambitious, but is common to all who are ill-used by fortune, and who are infirm in spirit. For a poor man also, who is miserly, will talk incessantly of the misuse of wealth and of the vices of the rich; whereby he merely torments himself, and shows the world that he is intolerant, not only of his own poverty, but also of other people's riches. So, again, those who have been ill received by a woman they love think of nothing but the inconstancy, treachery, and other stock faults of the fair sex; all of which they consign to oblivion, directly they are again taken into favor by their sweetheart.

Thus he who would govern his emotions and appetite solely by the love of freedom strives, as far as he can, to gain a knowledge of the virtues and their causes, and to fill his spirit with the joy which arises from the true knowledge of them: he will in no wise desire to dwell on men's faults, or to carp at his fellows, or to revel in a false show of freedom. *Whosoever will diligently observe and practice these precepts (which indeed are not difficult) will verily, in a short space of time, be able, for the most part, to direct his actions according to the commandments of reason.*

In proportion as a mental image is referred to more objects, so is it more frequent, or more often vivid, and occupies the mind more.

The mental images of things are more easily associated with the images referred to things which we clearly and distinctly understand, than with others.

A mental image is more often vivid, in proportion as it is associated with a greater number of other images.

The mind can bring it about that all bodily modifications or images of things may be referred to the idea of God.

He who clearly and distinctly understands himself and his emotions loves God, and so much the more in proportion as he more understands himself and his emotions.

This love toward God must hold the chief place in the mind.

God is without passions, neither is He affected by any emotion of pleasure or pain.

Strictly speaking, God does not love or hate anyone. For God is not affected by any emotion of pleasure or pain, consequently He does not love or hate anyone.

No one can hate God.

Love toward God cannot be turned into hate.

He who loves God cannot endeavor that God should love him in return.

This love toward God cannot be stained by the emotion of envy or jealousy: contrariwise, it is the more fostered in proportion as we conceive a greater number of men to be joined to God by the same bond of love.

We can in the same way show that there is no emotion directly contrary to this love, whereby this love can be destroyed; therefore we may conclude that this *love toward God is the most constant of all emotions*, and that, insofar as it is referred to the body, it cannot be destroyed unless the body be destroyed also. As to its nature, insofar as it is referred to the mind only, we shall presently inquire.

I have now gone through all the remedies against the emotions, or all that the mind, considered in itself alone, can do against them. Whence it appears that the mind's power over the emotions consists:—

I. In the actual knowledge of the emotions.

II. In the fact that it separates the emotions from the thought of an external cause, which we conceive confusedly.

III. In the fact that, in respect to time, the emotions referred to things which we distinctly understand surpass those referred to what we conceive in a confused and fragmentary manner.

IV. In the number of causes whereby those emotions are fostered which have regard to the common properties of things or to God.

V. Lastly, in the order wherein the mind can arrange and associate, one with another, its own emotions.

But, in order that this power of the mind over the emotions may be better understood it should be specially observed that the emotions are called by us strong, when we compare the emotion of one man with the emotion of another, and see that one man is more troubled than another by the same emotion; or when we are comparing the various emotions of the same man one with another, and find that he is more affected or stirred by one emotion than by another. For the strength of every emotion is defined by a comparison of our own power with the power of an external cause.

Now the power of the mind is defined by knowledge only, and its infirmity or passion is defined by the privation of knowledge only: it therefore follows that that mind is most passive whose greatest part is made up of inadequate ideas, so that it may be characterized more readily by its passive states than by its activities: on the other hand, that mind is most active whose greatest part is made up of adequate ideas, so that, although it may contain as many inadequate ideas as the former mind, it may yet be more easily characterized by ideas attributable to human virtue than by ideas which tell of human infirmity.

Again, it must be observed that spiritual unhealthiness and misfortunes can generally be traced to excessive love for something which is subject to many variations, and which we can never master. For no one is solicitous or anxious about anything unless he loves it; neither do wrongs, suspicions, enmities, etc. arise, except in regard to things whereof no one can be really master.

We may thus readily conceive the power which clear and distinct knowledge, and especially that third kind of knowledge, founded on the actual knowledge of God, possesses over the emotions: if it does not absolutely destroy them, insofar as they are passions; at any rate, it causes them to occupy a very small part of the mind.

Further, it begets a love toward a thing immutable and eternal, whereof we may really enter into possession; neither can it be defiled with those faults which are inherent in ordinary love; but it may grow from strength to strength, and may engross the greater part of the mind, and deeply penetrate it.

The mind can only imagine anything, or remember what is past, while the body endures.

Nevertheless in God there is necessarily an idea which expresses the essence of this or that human body under the form of eternity.

The human mind cannot be absolutely destroyed with the body, but there remains of it something which is eternal.

This idea, which expresses the essence of the body under the form of eternity, is, as we have said, a certain mode of thinking, which belongs to the essence of the mind, and is necessarily eternal. Yet it is not possible that we should remember that we existed before our body, for our body can bear no trace of such existence, neither can eternity be defined in terms of time, or have any relation to time.

But, notwithstanding, we feel and know that we are eternal. For the mind feels those things that it conceives by understanding, no less than those things that it remembers. For the eyes of the mind, whereby it sees and observes things, are none other than proofs. Thus, although we do not remember that we existed before the body, yet we feel that our mind, insofar as it involves the essence of the body, under the form of eternity, is eternal, and that thus its existence cannot be defined in terms of time, or explained through duration.

Thus our mind can only be said to endure, and its existence can only be defined by a fixed time, insofar as it involves the actual existence of the body. Thus far only has it the power of determining the existence of things by time, and conceiving them under the category of duration.

The more we understand particular things, the more do we understand God.

The highest endeavor of the mind, and the highest

virtue is to understand things by the intuitive kind of knowledge.

In proportion as the mind is more capable of understanding things by the intuitive kind of knowledge, it desires more to understand things by that kind.

From the intuitive kind of knowledge arises the highest possible mental acquiescence.

The endeavor or desire to know things by the intuitive kind of knowledge cannot arise from knowledge based solely on opinion or imagination, but from the universal kind of knowledge which is reason.

Whatsoever the mind understands under the form of eternity, it does not understand by virtue of conceiving the present actual existence of the body, but by virtue of conceiving the essence of the body under the form of eternity.

Things are conceived by us as actual in two ways; either as existing in relation to a given time and place, or as contained in God and following from the necessity of the divine nature. Whatsoever we conceive in this second way as true or real, we conceive under the form of eternity, and their ideas involve the eternal and infinite essence of God.

The Intellectual
Love of God

Our mind, insofar as it knows itself and the body under the form of eternity, has to that extent necessarily a knowledge of God, and knows that it is in God, and is conceived through God.

The intuitive kind of knowledge depends on the mind, as its formal cause, insofar as the mind itself is eternal.

In proportion, therefore, as a man is more potent in this kind of knowledge, he will be more completely conscious of himself and of God; in other words, he will be more perfect and blessed, as will appear more clearly shortly.

But we must here observe that, although we are already certain that the mind is eternal, insofar as it conceives things under the form of eternity, yet, in order that what we wish to show may be more readily explained and better understood, we will consider the mind itself, as though it had just begun to exist and to understand things under the form of eternity, as indeed we have done hitherto; this we may do without any danger of error, so long as we are careful not to draw any conclusion, unless our premises are plain.

Whatsoever we understand by the intuitive kind of knowledge, we take delight in, and our delight is accompanied by the idea of God as cause.

From the intuitive kind of knowledge necessarily arises the intellectual love of God. From this kind of knowledge, arises pleasure accompanied by the idea of God as cause, that is the love of God; not insofar as we understand Him to be eternal; this is what I call the intellectual love of God.

The intellectual love of God, which arises from the intuitive kind of knowledge, is eternal.

Although this love toward God has no beginning, it yet possesses all the perfections of love. Nor is there here any difference, except that the mind possesses as eternal those same perfections which we feigned to accrue to it, and they are accompanied by the idea of God as eternal cause. If pleasure consists in the transition to a greater perfection, assuredly blessedness must consist in the mind being endowed with perfection itself.

The mind is, only while the body endures, subject to those emotions which are attributable to passions.

No love save intellectual love is eternal.

If we look to men's general opinion, we shall see that they are indeed conscious of the eternity of

their mind, but that they confuse eternity with duration and ascribe it to the imagination or the memory which they believe to remain after death.

God loves Himself with an infinite intellectual
love.

The intellectual love of the mind toward God is
that very love of God whereby God loves Himself,
not insofar as He is infinite, but insofar as He can be
explained through the essence of the human mind
regarded under the form of eternity; in other words,
*the intellectual love of the mind toward God is part
of the infinite love wherewith God loves Himself.*

Hence it follows that God, insofar as He loves
Himself, loves man and, consequently, that *the love
of God toward men, and the intellectual love of the
mind toward God are identical.*

From what has been said we clearly understand
wherein our salvation, or blessedness, or freedom,
consists: namely, in the constant and eternal love
toward God, or in God's love toward men. This love
or blessedness is, in the Bible, called *Shechinah*
(Glory), and not undeservedly. For whether this
love be referred to God or to the mind, it may rightly
be called acquiescence of spirit, which is not really
distinguished from glory. Insofar as it is referred to
God, it is pleasure, if we may still use that term,
accompanied by the idea of itself, and, insofar as
it is referred to the mind, it is the same.

Again, since the essence of our mind consists solely in knowledge, whereof the beginning and the foundation is God, it becomes clear to us in what manner and way our mind, as to its essence and existence, follows from the divine nature and constantly depends on God.

I have thought it worth while here to call attention to this, in order to show by this example how the knowledge of particular things, which I have called intuitive, is potent, and more powerful than the universal knowledge, which I have styled reason.

There is nothing in nature which is contrary to this intellectual love, or which can take it away.

In proportion as the mind understands more things by the universal and intuitive kinds of knowledge, it is less subject to those emotions which are evil, and stands in less fear of death.

The Blessedness
of Inner Freedom

Death becomes less hurtful, in proportion as the mind's clear and distinct knowledge is greater, and, consequently, in proportion as the mind loves God more. Again, since from the intuitive kind of knowledge arises the highest possible acquiescence, it follows that the human mind can attain to being of such a nature that the part thereof which we have shown to perish with the body should be of little importance when compared with the part which endures.

He who possesses a body capable of the greatest number of activities, possesses a mind whereof the greatest part is eternal.

Since human bodies are capable of the greatest number of activities, there is no doubt but that they may be of such a nature that they may be referred to minds possessing a great knowledge of themselves and of God, and whereof the greatest or chief part part is eternal, and, therefore, that they should scarcely fear death. But, in order that this may be understood more clearly, we must here call to mind that we live in a state of perpetual variation, and, according as we are changed for the better or the worse, we are called happy or unhappy.

For he who, from being an infant or a child, becomes a corpse, is called unhappy; whereas it is set down to happiness, if we have been able to live through the whole period of life with a sound mind in a sound body. And, in reality, he who, as in the case of an infant or a child, has a body capable of very few activities, and depending, for the most part, on external causes, has a mind which, considered in itself alone, is scarcely conscious of itself, or of God, or of things; whereas he who has a body capable of very many activities, has a mind which, considered in itself alone, is highly conscious of itself, of God, and of things.

In this life, therefore, we primarily endeavor to bring it about that the body of a child, insofar as its nature allows and conduces thereto, may be changed into something else capable of very many activities, and referable to a mind which is highly conscious of itself, of God, and of things; and we desire so to change it that what is referred to its imagination and memory may become insignificant, in comparison with its intellect.

In proportion as each thing possesses more of perfection, so is it more active, and less passive; and, vice versa, in proportion as it is more active, so is it more perfect.

Hence it follows that the part of the mind which

endures, be it great or small, is more perfect than the rest. For the eternal part of the mind is the understanding, through which alone we are said to act; the part which we have shown to perish is the imagination, through which only we are said to be passive; therefore, the former, be it great or small, is more perfect than the latter.

Such are the doctrines which I had purposed to set forth concerning the mind, insofar as it is regarded without relation to the body; whence it is plain that our mind, insofar as it understands, is an eternal mode of thinking, which is determined by another mode of thinking, and this other by a third, and so on to infinity; so that all taken together at once constitute the eternal and infinite intellect of God.

Even if we did not know that our mind is eternal, we should still consider as of primary importance piety and religion, and generally all things attributable to courage and highmindedeness.

The general belief of the multitude seems to be peculiar. Most people seem to believe that they are free, insofar as they may obey their lusts, and that they cede their rights, insofar as they are bound to live according to the commandments of the divine law. They therefore believe that piety, religion, and, generally, all things attributable to firmness of mind, are burdens, which, after death, they hope to lay aside, and to receive the reward for their bondage, that is, for their piety and religion; it is not only by this hope, but also, and chiefly, by the fear of being horribly punished after death, that they are induced to live according to the divine commandments, so far as their feeble and infirm spirit will carry them.

If men had not this hope and this fear, but believed that the mind perishes with the body, and that no hope of prolonged life remains for the wretches who are broken down with the burden of piety, they would return to their inclinations, controlling everything in accordance with their lusts, and desiring to obey fortune rather than themselves.

Such a course appears to me not less absurd than if a man, because he does not believe that he can by wholesome food sustain his body forever, should wish to cram himself with poisons and deadly fare; or if, because he sees that the mind is not eternal or immortal, he should prefer to be out of his mind altogether, and to live without the use of reason; these ideas are so absurd as to be scarcely worth refuting.

Blessedness is not the reward of virtue, but virtue itself; neither do we rejoice therein, because we control our lusts, but, contrariwise, because we rejoice therein, we are able to control our lusts.

I have thus completed all I wished to set forth touching the mind's power over the emotions and the mind's freedom. Whence it appears *how potent is the wise man, and how much he surpasses the ignorant man, who is driven only by his lusts.* For the ignorant man is not only distracted in various ways by external causes without ever gaining the true acquiescence of his spirit, but moreover lives, as it were unwitting of himself, and of God, and of things, and as soon as he ceases to suffer, ceases also to be.

Whereas the wise man, insofar as he is regarded as such, is scarcely at all disturbed in spirit, but, being conscious of himself, and of God, and of things, by a certain eternal necessity, never ceases to be, but always possesses true acquiescence of his spirit.

If the way which I have pointed out as leading to this result seems exceedingly hard, it may nevertheless be discovered. Needs must it be hard, since it is so seldom found. How would it be possible, if salvation were ready to our hand, and could without great labor be found, that it should be by almost all men neglected? But all things excellent are as difficult as they are rare.

On God

God, or substance, consisting of infinite attributes, of which each expresses eternal and infinite essentiality, necessarily exists.

Besides God no substance can be granted or conceived.

Whatsoever is, is in God, and without God nothing can be, or be conceived.

From the necessity of the divine nature must follow an infinite number of things in infinite ways—that is, all things which can fall within the sphere of infinite intellect.

God is the indwelling and not the transient cause of all things.

The existence of God and His essence are one and the same.

God's existence, like His essence, is an eternal truth.

Individual things are nothing but modifications of the attributes of God, or forms by which the attributes of God are expressed in a fixed and definite manner.

Human Intellect in action finite or in action infinite can comprehend the attributes of God and the modifications of God and nothing else.

Every individual thing, or everything which is finite and has a conditioned existence, cannot exist or be conditioned to act, unless it be conditioned for existence and action by a cause other than itself, which also is finite, and has a conditioned existence; and likewise this cause cannot in its turn exist, or be conditioned to act, unless it be conditioned for existence and action by another cause, which also is finite, and has a conditioned existence, and so on to infinity.

Nothing in the universe is contingent, but all things are conditioned to exist and operate in a particular manner by the necessity of the divine nature.

Will cannot be called a free cause, but only a necessary cause.

God does not act according to freedom of the will.

Will and intellect stand in the same relation to the nature of God as do motion, and rest, and absolutely all natural phenomena, which must be conditioned by God to exist and act in a particular manner. For will, like the rest, stands in need of a cause, by which it is conditioned to exist and act in a particular manner. And although, when will or intellect be granted, an infinite number of results may follow, yet God cannot on that account be said to act from freedom of the will, any more than the infinite number of results from motion and rest would justify us in saying that motion and rest act by free will. Wherefore will no more appertains to God than does anything else in nature, but stands in the same relation to him as motion, rest, and the like, which follow from the necessity of the divine nature, and are conditioned by it to exist and act in a particular manner.

God is, and acts solely by the necessity of His own nature; He is the free cause of all things. All things are in God, and so depend on him, and without Him they could neither exist nor be conceived; lastly, all things are predetermined by God, not through His free will or absolute wish, but from the very nature of God or infinite power.

Yet there remain misconceptions not a few, which might and may prove very grave hindrances to the understanding of the concatenation of things. I have thought it worth while to bring these misconceptions before the bar of reason.

All such opinions spring from the notion commonly entertained that all things in nature act as men themselves act, namely, with an end in view. It is accepted as certain that God Himself directs all things to a definite goal (for it is said that God made all things for man, and man that he might worship Him). I will, therefore, consider this opinion, asking first, why it obtains general credence, and why all men are naturally so prone to adopt it? secondly, I will point out its falsity; and, lastly, I will show how it has given rise to prejudices about good and bad, right and wrong, praise and blame, order and confusion, beauty and ugliness, and the like. However, this is not the place to deduce these misconceptions from the nature of the human mind.

All men are born ignorant of the causes of things, all have the desire to seek for what is useful to them, and they are conscious of such desire. Herefrom it follows, first, that men think themselves free inasmuch as they are conscious of their volitions and desires, and never even dream, in their ignorance, of the causes which have disposed them so to wish and desire. Secondly, that men do all things for an end, namely, for that which is useful to them, and which they seek. Thus it comes to pass that they only look for a knowledge of the final causes of events, and when these are learned, they are content, as having no cause for further doubt. If they cannot learn such causes from external sources, they are compelled to turn to considering themselves, and reflecting what end would have induced them personally to bring about the given event, and thus they necessarily judge other natures by their own. Further, as they find in themselves and outside themselves many means which assist them not a little in their search for what is useful, for instance, eyes for seeing, teeth for chewing, herbs and animals for yielding food, the sun for giving light, the sea for breeding fish, etc., they come to look on the whole of nature as a means for obtaining such conveniences. Now as they are aware that they found these conveniences and did not make them, they think they have cause for believing that some other being has made them for their use.

As they look upon things as means, they cannot believe them to be self-created; but, judging from the means which they are accustomed to prepare for themselves, they are bound to believe in some ruler or rulers of the universe endowed with human freedom, who have arranged and adapted everything for human use. They are bound to estimate the nature of such rulers (having no information on the subject) in accordance with their own nature, and therefore they assert that the gods ordained everything for the use of man, in order to bind man to themselves and obtain from him the highest honor.

Hence also it follows that everyone thought out for himself, according to his abilities, a different way of worshiping God, so that God might love him more than his fellows, and direct the whole course of nature for the satisfaction of his blind cupidity and insatiable avarice. Thus the prejudice developed into superstition, and took deep root in the human mind; and for this reason everyone strove most zealously to understand and explain the final causes of things; but in their endeavor to show that nature does nothing in vain, *i.e.*, nothing which is useless to man, they only seem to have demonstrated that nature, the gods, and men are all mad together.

Consider, I pray you, the result: among the many helps of nature they were bound to find some hindrances, such as storms, earthquakes, diseases, etc.: so they declared that such things happen because the gods are angry at some wrong done them by men, or at some fault committed in their worship. Experience day by day protested and showed by infinite examples that good and evil fortunes fall to the lot of pious and impious alike; still they would not abandon their inveterate prejudice, for it was more easy for them to class such contradictions among other unknown things of whose use they were ignorant, and thus to retain their actual and innate condition of ignorance, than to destroy the whole fabric of their reasoning and start afresh.

They therefore laid down as an axiom, that God's judgments far transcend human understanding. Such a doctrine might well have sufficed to conceal the truth from the human race for all eternity, if mathematics had not furnished another standard of verity in considering solely the essence and properties of figures without regard to their final causes. There are other reasons (which I need not mention here) besides mathematics, which might have caused men's minds to be directed to these general prejudices, and have led them to the knowledge of the truth.

I have now explained my first point. There is no need to show at length that *nature has no particular goal in view, and final causes are mere human figments.* However, I will add a few remarks in order to overthrow the doctrine of a final cause utterly.

This doctrine does away with the perfection of God: for, if God acts for an object, He necessarily desires something which He lacks. Certainly, theologians and metaphysicians draw a distinction between the object of want and the object of assimilation; still they confess that God made all things for the sake of Himself, not for the sake of creation. They are unable to point to anything prior to creation, except God Himself, as an object for which God should act, and are therefore driven to admit (as they clearly must), that God lacked those things for whose attainment He created means, and further that He desired them.

We must not omit to notice that the followers of this doctrine, anxious to display their talent in assigning final causes, have imported a new method of argument in proof of their theory—namely, a reduction, not to the impossible, but to ignorance; thus showing that they have no other method of exhibiting their doctrine. For example, if a stone falls from a roof onto someone's head, and kills him, they will demonstrate by their new method that the stone fell in order to kill the man; for, if it had not by God's will fallen with that object, how could so many circumstances (and there are often many concurrent circumstances) have all happened together by chance? Perhaps you will answer that the event is due to the facts that the wind was blowing, and the man was walking that way. "But why," they will insist, "was the wind blowing, and why was the man at the very time walking that way?"

If you again answer, that the wind had then sprung up because the sea had begun to be agitated the day before, the weather being previously calm, and that the man had been invited by a friend, they will again insist: "But why was the sea agitated, and why was the man invited at that time?" So they will pursue their questions from cause to cause, till at last you take refuge in the will of God—in other words, the sanctuary of ignorance. So, again, when they survey the frame of the human body, they are amazed; and being ignorant of the causes of so great a work of art, conclude that it has been fashioned, not mechanically, but by divine and supernatural skill, and has been so put together that one part shall not hurt another.

Hence anyone who seeks for the true causes of miracles, and strives to understand natural phenomena as an intelligent being, and not to gaze at them like a fool, is set down and denounced as an impious heretic by those whom the masses adore as the interpreters of nature and the gods. Such persons know that, with the removal of ignorance, the wonder which forms their only available means for proving and preserving their authority would vanish also. But I now quit this subject, and pass on to my third point.

After men persuaded themselves that everything which is created is created for their sake, they were bound to consider as the chief quality in everything that which is most useful to themselves, and to account those things the best of all which have the most beneficial effect on mankind. Further, they were bound to form abstract notions for the explanation of the nature of things, such as goodness, badness, order, confusion, warmth, cold, beauty, deformity, and so on; and from the belief that they are free agents arose the further notions, praise and blame, sin and merit.

Everything which conduces to health and the worship of God they have called good, everything which hinders these objects they have styled bad; and inasmuch as those who do not understand the nature of things do not verify phenomena in any way, but merely imagine them after a fashion, and mistake their imagination for understanding, such persons firmly believe that there is an order in things, being really ignorant both of things and their own nature.

When phenomena are of such a kind that the impression they make on our senses requires little effort of imagination, and can consequently be easily remembered, we say that they are well-ordered; if the contrary, that they are ill ordered or confused. Further, as things which are easily imagined are more pleasing to us, men prefer order to confusion —as though there were any order in nature, except in relation to our imagination—and say that God has created all things in order; thus, without knowing it, attributing imagination to God, unless, indeed, they would have it that God foresaw human imagination, and arranged everything so that it should be most easily imagined.

If this be their theory, they would not, perhaps, be daunted by the fact that we find an infinite number of phenomena, far surpassing our imagination, and very many others which confound its weakness.

The other abstract notions are nothing but modes of imagining, in which the imagination is differently affected, though they are considered by the ignorant as the chief attributes of things, inasmuch as they believe that everything was created for the sake of themselves; and, according as they are affected by it, style it good or bad, healthy or rotten and corrupt. For instance, if the motion which objects we see communicate to our nerves be conducive to health, the objects causing it are styled beautiful; if a contrary motion be excited, they are styled ugly.

Things which are perceived through our sense of smell are styled fragrant or fetid; if through our taste, sweet or bitter, full-flavored or insipid; if through our touch, hard or soft, rough or smooth, etc.

Whatsoever affects our ears is said to give rise to noise, sound, or harmony. In this last case, there are men lunatic enough to believe that even God Himself takes pleasure in harmony; and philosophers are not lacking who have persuaded themselves that the motion of the heavenly bodies gives rise to harmony —all of which instances sufficiently show that everyone judges of things according to the state of his brain, or rather mistakes for things the forms of his imagination. We need no longer wonder that there have arisen all the controversies we have witnessed, and finally skepticism: for, although human bodies in many respects agree, yet in very many others they differ; so that what seems good to one seems bad to another; what is pleasing to one displeases another, and so on.

I need not further enumerate, because the fact is sufficiently well known. It is commonly said: "So many men, so many minds; everyone is wise in his own way; brains differ as completely as palates." All of which proverbs show that men judge of things according to their mental disposition, and rather imagine than understand: for, if they understood phenomena, they would, as mathematics attest, be convinced, if not attracted, by what I have urged.

All the explanations commonly given of nature are mere modes of imagining, and do not indicate the true nature of anything, but only the constitution of the imagination; and, although they have names, as though they were entities, existing externally in

179

the imagination, I call them entities imaginary rather than real; and, therefore, all arguments against us drawn from abstractions are easily rebutted.

Many argue in this way. If all things follow from a necessity of the absolutely perfect nature of God, why are there so many imperfections in nature? such, for instance, as things corrupt to the point of putridity, loathsome deformity, confusion, evil, sin etc. But these reasoners are, as I have said, easily confuted, for the perfection of things is to be reckoned only from their own nature and power; things are not more or less perfect, according as they delight or offend human senses, or according as they are serviceable or repugnant to mankind. To those who ask why God did not so create all men that they should be governed only by reason, I give no answer but this: because matter was not lacking to Him for the creation of every degree of perfection from highest to lowest; or, more strictly, because the laws of His nature are so vast as to suffice for the production of everything conceivable by an infinite intelligence.

Such are the misconceptions I have undertaken to note; if there are any more of the same sort, everyone may easily dissipate them for himself with the aid of a little reflection.

On the Nature and Origin of the Mind

Ideas, Things, and the Human Mind

By body I mean a mode or created form which expresses in a certain determinate manner the essence of God, insofar as He is considered as an extended thing. I consider as belonging to the essence of a thing that which, being given, the thing is necessarily given also, and which, being removed, the thing is necessarily removed also; in other words, that without which the thing, and which itself without the thing, can neither be nor be conceived.

By idea, I mean the mental conception which is formed by the mind as a thinking thing. I say conception rather than perception, because the word perception seems to imply that the mind is passive in respect to the object; whereas conception seems to express an activity of the mind.

By an adequate idea, I mean an idea which, insofar as it is considered in itself, without relation to the object, has all the properties or intrinsic marks of a true idea. I say intrinsic, in order to exclude that mark which is extrinsic, namely, the agreement between the idea and its object.

Duration is the indefinite continuance of existing. I say indefinite, because it cannot be determined through the existence itself of the existing thing, or by its efficient cause, which necessarily gives the existence of the thing, but does not take it away. Reality and perfection I use as synonymous terms.

By particular things, I mean things which are finite and have a conditioned existence; but if several individual things concur in one action, so as to be all simultaneously the effect of one cause, I consider them all, so far, as one particular thing.

Thought is an attribute of God, or God is a thinking thing.

Extension is an attribute of God, or God is an extended thing.

The idea of God, from which an infinite number of things follow in infinite ways, can only be one.

Infinite intellect comprehends nothing save the attributes of God and his modifications. Now God is one. Therefore the idea of God, wherefrom an infinite number of things follow in infinite ways, can only be one.

The order and connection of ideas is the same as the order and connection of things.

Whatsoever can be perceived by the infinite intellect as constituting the essence of substance, belongs altogether only to one substance: consequently, substance *thinking* and substance *extended* are one and the same substance, comprehended now through one attribute, now through the other. So, also, a mode of extension and the idea of that mode are one and the same thing, though expressed in two ways. This truth seems to have been dimly recognized by those Jews who maintained that God, God's intellect, and the things understood by God are identical.

For instance, a circle existing in nature, and the idea of a circle existing, which is also in God, are one and the same thing displayed through different attributes. Thus, whether we conceive nature under the attribute of extension, or under the attribute of thought, or under any other attribute, we shall find the same order, or one and the same chain of causes —that is, the same things following in either case.

I said that God is the cause of an idea—for instance, of the idea of a circle—insofar as he is a thinking thing; and of a circle, insofar as he is an extended thing, simply because the actual being of the idea of a circle can only be perceived as a proximate cause through another mode of thinking, and that again through another, and so on to infinity. So long as we consider things as modes of thinking, we must explain the order of the whole of nature, or the whole chain of causes, through the attribute of thought only. And, insofar as we consider things as modes of extension, we must explain the order of

the whole of nature through the attribute of extension only; and so on, in the case of other attributes.

Wherefore of things as they are in themselves God
is really the cause, inasmuch as he consists of infinite
attributes.

The first element, which constitutes the actual
being of the human mind, is the idea of some particular thing actually existing.

The human mind is part of the infinite intellect of
God; thus when we say that the human mind perceives this or that, we make the assertion that God
has this or that idea, not insofar as He is infinite, but
insofar as He is displayed through the nature of the
human mind, or insofar as He constitutes the essence
of the human mind; and when we say that God has
this or that idea, not only insofar as He constitutes
the essences of the human mind, but also insofar as
He, simultaneously with the human mind, has the
further idea of another thing, we assert that the human mind perceives a thing in part or inadequately.

The object of the idea constituting the human
mind is the body, in other words a certain mode of
extension which actually exists, and nothing else.

We comprehend, not only that the human mind is
united to the body, but also the nature of the union
between mind and body. However, no one will be
able to grasp this adequately or distinctly unless he

first has adequate knowledge of the nature of our body. The propositions we have advanced hitherto have been entirely general, applying not more to men than to other individual things, all of which, though in different degrees, are animated. For of everything there is necessarily an idea in God, of which God is the cause, in the same way as there is an idea of the human body; thus whatever we have asserted of the idea of the human body must necessarily also be asserted of the idea of everything else. Still, on the other hand, we cannot deny that ideas, like objects, differ one from the other, one being more excellent than another and containing more reality, just as the object of one idea is more excellent than the object of another idea, and contains more reality.

Wherefore, in order to determine wherein the human mind differs from other things, and wherein it surpasses them, it is necessary for us to know the nature of its object, that is, of the human body. What this nature is, I am not able here to explain, nor is it necessary for the proof of what I advance, that I should do so. I will only say generally, that in proportion as any given body is more fitted than others for doing many actions or receiving many impressions at once, so also is the mind, of which it is the object, more fitted than others for forming many simultaneous perceptions; and the more the actions of one body depend on itself alone, and the fewer other bodies concur with it in action, the more fitted is the mind of which it is the object for distinct comprehension.

We may thus recognize the superiority of one mind over others, and may further see the cause, why we have only a very confused knowledge of our body, and also many kindred questions.

All bodies are either in motion or at rest.

Every body is moved sometimes more slowly, sometimes more quickly.

Bodies are distinguished from one another in respect of motion and rest, quickness and slowness, and not in respect of substance.

A body in motion or at rest must be determined to motion or rest by another body, which other body has been determined to motion or rest by a third body, and that third again by a fourth, and so on to infinity.

A body in motion keeps in motion, until it is determined to a state of rest by some other body; and a body at rest remains so, until it is determined to a state of motion by some other body. This is indeed self-evident. For when I suppose, for instance, that a given body, A, is at rest, and do not take into consideration other bodies in motion, I cannot affirm anything concerning the body A, except that it is at rest. If it afterwards comes to pass that A is in motion, this cannot have resulted from its having been at rest, for no other consequence could have been involved than its remaining at rest. If, on the other hand, A be given in motion, we shall, so long as we only consider A, be unable to affirm anything concerning it, except that it is in motion. If A is subsequently found to be at rest, this rest cannot be the result of A's previous motion, for such motion can only have led to continued motion; the state of rest therefore must have resulted from something, which was not in A, namely, from an external cause determining A to a state of rest.

All modes wherein one body is affected by another body follow simultaneously from the nature of the body affected and the body affecting, so that one and the same body may be moved in different modes, according to the difference in the nature of the bodies moving it; on the other hand, different bodies may be moved in different modes by one and the same body.

When a body in motion impinges on another body at rest, which it is unable to move, it recoils, in order to continue its motion, and the angle made by the line of motion in the recoil and the plane of the body at rest, whereon the moving body has impinged, will be equal to the angle formed by the line of motion of incidence and the same plane.

When any given bodies of the same or different magnitude are compelled by other bodies to remain in contact, or if they be moved at the same or different rates of speed, so that their mutual movements should preserve among themselves a certain fixed relation, we say that such bodies are in union, and that altogether they compose one body or individual, which is distinguished from other bodies by this fact of union.

In proportion as the parts of an individual, or a compound body, are in contact over a greater or less superficies, they will with greater or less difficulty admit of being moved from their position; consequently the individual will, with greater or less difficulty, be brought to assume another form. Those bodies, whose parts are in contact over large superficies, are called *hard;* those, whose parts are in contact over small superficies, are called *soft;* those, whose parts are in motion among one another, are called *fluid.*

If certain bodies composing an individual be compelled to change the motion which they have in one direction for motion in another direction, but in such a manner that they be able to continue their motions and their mutual communication in the same relations as before, the individual will retain its own nature without any change of its actuality.

Furthermore, the individual thus composed preserves its nature, whether it be, as a whole, in motion or at rest, whether it be moved in this or that direction; so long as each part retains its motion, and preserves its communication with other parts as before.

A composite individual may be affected in many different ways, and preserve its nature notwithstanding. Thus far we have conceived an individual as composed of several individuals of diverse natures, other in respect of motion and rest, speed and slowness; that is, of bodies of the most simple character. If, however, we now conceive another individual composed of several individuals of diverse natures, we shall find that the number of ways in which it can be affected, without losing its nature, will be greatly multiplied. Each of its parts would consist of several bodies, and therefore each part would admit, without change to its nature, of quicker or slower motion, and would consequently be able to transmit its motions more quickly or more slowly to the remaining parts. If we further conceive a third kind of individuals composed of individuals of this second kind, we shall find that they may be affected in a still greater number of ways without changing their actuality.

We may easily proceed thus to infinity, and conceive the whole of nature as one individual, whose parts, that is, all bodies, vary in infinite ways, without any change in the individual as a whole.

The human mind is capable of perceiving a great number of things, and is so in proportion as its body is capable of receiving a great number of impressions.

The idea which constitutes the actual being of

the human mind, is not simple, but compounded of a great number of ideas.

The idea of every mode, in which the human body is affected by external bodies, must involve the nature of the human body, and also the nature of the external body.

The human mind perceives the nature of a variety of bodies, together with the nature of its own.

The ideas which we have of external bodies indicate rather the constitution of our own body than the nature of external bodies.

If the human body is affected in a manner which involves the nature of any external body, the human mind will regard the said external body as actually existing, or as present to itself, until the human body be affected in such a way as to exclude the existence or the presence of the said external body.

The human mind does not perceive any external body as actually existing, except through the ideas of the modifications of its own body.

The human mind has no knowledge of the body, and does not know it to exist, save through the ideas of the modifications through which the body is affected.

The mind does not know itself, except insofar as it perceives the ideas of the modifications of the body.

The human mind does not involve an adequate knowledge of the parts composing the human body.

We can ony have a very inadequate knowledge of the duration of our body.

All ideas, insofar as they are referred to God, are true.

All ideas which are in God agree in every respect with their objects; therefore they are all true.

Every idea, which in us is absolute or adequate and perfect, is true.

When we say that an idea in us is adequate and perfect, we say, in other words, that the idea is adequate and perfect in God, insofar as he constitutes the essence of our mind; consequently, we say that such an idea is true.

Falsity consists in the privation of knowledge, which inadequate, fragmentary, or confused ideas involve.

Inadequate and confused ideas follow by the same necessity, and adequate or clear and distinct ideas.

All ideas are in God, and insofar as they are referred to God are true and adequate; therefore there are no ideas confused or inadequate, except in respect to a particular mind; therefore all ideas, whether adequate or inadequate, follow by the same necessity.

Whatsoever ideas in the mind follow from ideas which are therein adequate, are also themselves adequate.

For when we say that an idea in the human mind follows from ideas which are therein adequate, we say, in other words, that an idea is in the divine intellect, whereof God is the cause, not insofar as He is infinite, nor insofar as He is affected by the ideas of very many particular things, but only insofar as He constitutes the essence of the human mind.

The Three Ways
of Knowing

I will briefly set down the causes whence are derived the terms styled *transcendental,* such as Being, Thing, Something. These terms arose from the fact that the human body, being limited, is only capable of distinctly forming a certain number of images within itself at the same time; if this number be exceeded, the images will begin to be confused; if this number of images, which the body is capable of forming distinctly within itself, be largely exceeded, all will become entirely confused one with another.

This being so, it is evident that the human mind can distinctly imagine as many things simultaneously as its body can form images simultaneously. When the images become quite confused in the body, the mind also imagines all bodies confusedly without any distinction, and will comprehend them, as it were, under one attribute, namely, under the attribute of Being, Thing, etc. The same conclusion can be drawn from the fact that images are not always equally vivid, and from other analogous causes, which there is no need to explain here; for the purpose which we have in view it is sufficient for us to consider one only.

All may be reduced to this, that these terms represent ideas in the highest degree confused. From similar causes arise those notions, which we call *general*, such as man, horse, dog, etc. They arise, to wit, from the fact that so many images, for instance, of men, are formed simultaneously in the human mind that the powers of imagination break down, not indeed utterly, but to the extent of the mind losing count of small differences betwen individuals (*e.g.* color, size, etc.) and their definite number, and only distinctly imagining that in which all the individulas, insofar as the body is afffected by them, agree; for that is the point in which each of the said individuals chiefly affected the body; this the mind expresses by the name man, and this it predicates of an infinite number of particular individuals.

For, as we have said, it is unable to imagine the definite number of individuals. We must, however, bear in mind that these general notions are not formed by all men in the same way, but vary in each individual according as the point varies, whereby the body has been most often affected and which the mind most easily imagines or remembers. For instance, those who have most often regarded with admiration the stature of man, will by the name of man understand an animal of erect stature; those who have been accustomed to regard some other attribute, will form a different general image of man, for instance, that man is a laughing animal, a two-footed animal without feathers, a rational animal, and thus, in other cases, everyone will form general images of things according to the habit of his body.

It is thus not to be wondered at, that among philosophers, who seek to explain things in nature merely by the images formed of them, so many controversies should have arisen.

From all that has been said above it is clear that we, in many cases, perceive and form our general notions:—(1.) From particular things represented to our intellect fragmentarily, confusedly, and without order through our senses; I have settled to call such perceptions by the name of knowledge from the mere suggestions of experience. (2.) From symbols, *e.g.*, from the fact of having read or heard certain words, we remember things and form certain ideas concerning them, similar to those through which we imagine things. I shall call both these ways of regarding things *knowledge of the first kind, opinion,* or *imagination.* (3.) From the fact that we have notions common to all men, and adequate ideas of the properties of things; this I call *reason* and *knowledge of the second kind.* Besides these two kinds of knowledge, there is the third kind of knowledge, which we call *intuition.* This kind of knowledge proceeds from an adequate idea of the absolute essence of certain attributes of God to the adequate knowledge of the essence of things.

Knowledge of the first kind is the only source of falsity, knowledge of the second and third kinds is necessarily true.

He who has a true idea simultaneously knows that he has a true idea, and cannot doubt of the truth of the thing perceived.

It is not in the nature of reason to regard things as contingent, but as necessary.

It is in the nature of reason to perceive things under a certain form of eternity.

Although each particular thing be conditioned by another particular thing to exist in a given way, yet the force whereby each particular thing perseveres in existing follows from the eternal necessity of God's nature.

The knowledge of the eternal and infinite essence of God which every idea involves is adequate and perfect.

We see that the infinite essence and the eternity of God are known to all. Now as all things are in God, and are conceived through God, we can from this knowledge infer many things which we may adequately know, and we may form that third kind of knowledge of which we spoke, and of the excellence and use of which we shall have occasion to speak again.

Men have not so clear a knowledge of God as they have of general notions, because they are unable to imagine God as they do bodies, and also because they associated the name God with images of things that they are in the habit of seeing, as indeed they can hardly avoid doing, being, as they are, men, and continually affected by external bodies.

Many errors, in truth, can be traced to this head, namely, that we do not apply names to things rightly. For instance, when a man says that the lines drawn from the center of a circle to its circumference are not equal, he then, at all events, assuredly attaches a meaning to the word circle different from that assigned by mathematicians. So again, when men make mistakes in calculation, they have one set of figures in their mind, and another on the paper.

If we could see into their minds, they do not make a mistake; they seem to do so, because we think that they have the same numbers in their mind as they have on the paper. If this were not so, we should not believe them to be in error, any more than I thought that a man was in error whom I lately heard exclaiming that his entrance hall had flown into a neighbour's hen, for his meaning seemed to me sufficiently clear. *Very many controversies have arisen from the fact that men do not rightly explain their meaning, or do not rightly in-*

terpret the meaning of others. For, as a matter of fact, as they flatly contradict themselves, they assume now one side, now another, of the argument, so as to oppose the opinions which they consider mistaken and absurd in their opponents.

In the mind there is no absolute or free will; but the mind is determined to wish this or that by a cause, which has also been determined by another cause, and this last by another cause, and so on to infinity.

Will and understanding are one and the same.

Will
and Virtue

I wish my readers to make an accurate distinction between an idea, or concept of the mind, and the images of things which we imagine. It is further necessary that they should distinguish between ideas and words, whereby we signify things. These three—namely, images, words, and ideas—are by many persons either entirely confused together, or not distinguished with sufficient accuracy or care, and hence people are generally in ignorance how absolutely necessary is a knowledge of this doctrine of the will, both for philosophic purposes and for the wise ordering of life.

Those who think that ideas consist in images which are formed in us by contact with external bodies, persuade themselves that the ideas of those things, whereof we can form no mental picture, are not ideas, but only figments, which we invent by the free decree of our will; they thus regard ideas as though they were inanimate pictures on a panel, and, filled with this misconception, do not see that an idea, inasmuch as it is an idea, involves an affirmation or negation. Again, those who confuse idea involves, think that they can wish something contrary to what they feel, affirm, or deny.

This misconception will easily be laid aside by one who reflects on the nature of knowledge, and seeing that it in no wise involves the conception of words with ideas, or with the affirmation which an extension, will therefore clearly understand that an idea (being a mode of thinking) does not consist in the image of anything, nor in words. The essence of words and images is put together by bodily motions, which in no wise involve the concept of thought.

These few words on this subject will suffice: I will therefore pass on to consider the objections, which may be raised against our doctrine. Of these, the first is advanced by those who think that the will has a wider scope than the understanding, and that therefore it is different therefrom. The reason for their holding the belief that the will has wider scope than the understanding, is that they assert that they have no need of an increase in their faculty of assent, that is of affirmation or negation, in order to assent to an infinity of things which we do not perceive, but that they have need of an increase in their faculty of understanding.

The will is thus distinguished from the intellect, the latter being finite and the former infinite. Secondly, it may be objected that experience seems to teach us especially clearly that we are able to suspend our judgement before assenting to things which we perceive; this is confirmed by the fact that no one is said to be deceived, insofar as he perceives anything, but only insofar as he assents or dissents.

For instance, he who feigns a winged horse, does not therefore admit that a winged horse exists; that is, he is not deceived, unless he admits in addition that a winged horse does exist. Nothing therefore seems to be taught more clearly by experience, than that the will or faculty of assent is free and different from the faculty of understanding. Thirdly, it may be objected that one affirmation does not apparently contain more reality than another; in other words, that we do not seem to need for affirming that what is true is true, any greater power than for affirming that what is false is true.

We have, however, seen that one idea has more reality or perfection than another, for as objects some are more excellent than others; this also seems to point to a difference between the understanding and the will.

Fourthly, it may be objected, if man does not act from free will, what will happen if the incentives to action are equally balanced, as in the case of Buridan's ass? Will he perish of hunger and thirst? If I say that he would, I shall seem to have in my thoughts an ass or the statue of a man rather than an actual man. If I say that he would not, he would

then determine his own action, and would consequently possess the faculty of going and doing whatever he liked. Other objections might also be raised,
but, as I am not bound to put in evidence everything
that anyone may dream, I will only set myself to the
task of refuting those I have mentioned, and that as
briefly as possible.

To the *first* objection I answer that I admit that
the will has a wider scope than the understanding, if
by the understanding be meant only clear and distinct ideas; but I deny that the will has a wider scope
than the perceptions, and the faculty of forming
conceptions; nor do I see why the faculty of volition
should be called infinite, any more than the faculty
of feeling: for, as we are able by the same faculty of
volition to affirm an infinite number of things (one
after the other, for we cannot affirm an infinite number simultaneously), so also can we, by the same
faculty of feeling, feel or perceive (in succession) an
infinite number of bodies.

If it be said that there is an infinite number of
things which we cannot perceive, I answer that we
cannot attain to such things by any thinking, nor,
consequently, by any faculty of volition. But, it may
still be urged, if God wished to bring it about that
we should perceive them, He would be obliged to
endow us with a greater faculty of perception, but
not a greater faculty of volition than we have already. This is the same as to say that, if God wished
to bring it about that we should understand an in-

finite number of other entities, it would be necessary for Him to give us a greater understanding, but not a more universal idea of entity than that which we have already, in order to grasp such infinite entities. We have shown that will is a universal entity or idea, whereby we explain all particular volitions—in other words, that which is common to all such volitions.

As, then, our opponents maintain that this idea, common or universal to all volitions, is a faculty, it is little to be wondered at that they assert that such a faculty extends itself into the infinite, beyond the limits of the understanding: for what is universal is predicated alike of one, of many, and of an infinite number of individuals.

To the *second* objection I reply by denying that we have a free power of suspending our judgment: for, when we say that anyone suspends his judgment, we merely mean that he sees, that he does not perceive the matter in question adequately.

Suspension of judgment is, therefore, strictly speaking, a perception, and not free will. In order to illustrate the point, let us suppose a boy imagining a horse, and perceiving nothing else. Inasmuch as this imagination involves the existence of the horse, and the boy does not perceive anything which would exclude the existence of the horse, he will necesarily regard the horse as present: he will not be able to doubt of its existence, although he be not certain thereof. We have daily experience of such a state of things in dreams; and I do not suppose that there is anyone who would maintain that, while he is dreaming, he has the free power of suspending his judgment concerning the things in his dream, and bringing it about that he should not dream those things, which he dreams that he sees; yet it happens, notwithstanding, that even in dreams we suspend our judgment, namely, when we dream that we are dreaming.

Further, I grant that no one can be deceived, so far as actual perception extends—that is, I grant that the mind's imaginations, regarded in themselves, do not involve error; but I deny that a man does not, in the act of perception, make any affirmation. For what is the perception of a winged horse, save affirming that a horse has wings?

If the mind could perceive nothing else but the winged horse, it would regard the same as present to itself: it would have no reasons for doubting its existence, nor any faculty of dissent, unless the imagination of a winged horse be joined to an idea which precludes the existence of the said horse, or unless the mind perceives that the idea which it possesses of a winged horse is inadequate, in which case it will either necessarily deny the existence of such a horse, or will necessarily be in doubt on the subject.

I think that I have anticipated my answer to the *third* objection, namely, that the will is something universal which is predicated of all ideas, and that it only signifies that which is common to all ideas, namely, an affirmation, whose adequate essence must, therefore, insofar as it is thus conceived in the abstract, be in every idea, and be, in this respect alone, the same in all, not insofar as it is considered as constituting the idea's essence: for, in this respect, particular affirmations differ one from the other, as much as do ideas. For instance, the affirmation which involves the idea of a circle, differs from that which involves the idea of a triangle, as much as the idea of a circle differs from the idea of a triangle.

Further, I absolutely deny that we are in need of an equal power of thinking to affirm that that which is true is true, and to affirm that that which is false is true. These two affirmations, if we regard the mind, are in the same relation to one another as being and not-being; for there is nothing positive in ideas which constitutes the actual reality of falsehood.

We must therefore conclude that we are easily deceived, when we confuse universals with singulars, and the entities of reason and abstractions with realities. As for the *fourth* objection, I am quite ready to admit that a man placed in the equilibrium described (namely, as perceiving nothing but hunger and thirst, a certain food and a certain drink, each equally distant from him) would die of hunger and thirst. If I am asked whether such a one should not rather be considered an ass than a man; I answer, that I do not know, neither do I know how a man should be considered who hangs himself, or how we should consider children, fools, madmen, etc.

It remains to point out the advantages of a knowledge of this doctrine as bearing on conduct, and this may be easily gathered from what has been said. The doctrine is good,

1. Inasmuch as it teaches us to act solely according to the decree of God, and to be partakers in the Divine nature, and so much the more, as we perform more perfect actions and more and more understand God. Such a doctrine not only completely tranquillizes our spirit, but also shows us where our highest happiness or blessedness is, namely, solely in the knowledge of God, whereby we are led to act only as love and piety shall bid us.

We may thus clearly understand how far astray from a true estimate of virtue are those who expect to be decorated by God with high rewards for their virtue, and their best actions, as for having endured the direst slavery; as if virtue and the service of God were not in itself happiness and perfect freedom.

2. Inasmuch as it teaches us how we ought to conduct ourselves with respect to the gifts of fortune, or matters which are not in our own power, and do not follow from our nature. For it shows us that we should await and endure fortune's smiles or frowns with an equal mind, seeing that all things

follow from the eternal decree of God by the same necessity as it follows from the essence of a triangle that the three angles are equal to two right angles.

3. This doctrine raises social life, inasmuch as it teaches us to hate no man, neither to despise, to deride, to envy, or to be angry with any. Further, as it tells us that each should be content with his own, and helpful to his neighbour, not from any womanish pity, favor, or superstition, but solely by the guidance of reason.

4. Lastly, this doctrine confers no small advantage on the commonwealth; for it teaches how citizens should be governed and led, not so as to become slaves, but so that they may freely do whatsoever things are best.

ACKNOWLEDGMENT

PASSIONS AND INTELLIGENCE

Part V: Of the Power of the Understanding, or of Human Freedom

Propositions 1, 2, 3, 4, 5, 6, 7, 8, 9, 10, 11, 12, 13, 14, 15, 16, 17, 18, 19, 20

THE STRENGTH OF THE MIND

Part V: Propositions 20, 21, 22, 23, 24, 25, 26, 27, 28, 29

THE INTELLECTUAL LOVE OF GOD

Part V: Propositions 30, 31, 32, 33, 34, 35, 36, 37, 38

THE BLESSEDNESS OF INNER FREEDOM

Part V: Propositions 38, 39, 40, 41, 42

THE GOD THAT IS

Part I: Concerning God

Propositions 11, 14, 15, 16, 18, 20, 25, 30, 28, 29, 32

THE GOD OF MAN'S MAKING

Part I: Appendix

IDEAS, THINGS, AND THE HUMAN MIND

Part II: Of the Nature and Origin of the Mind

Definitions, 1-7; Propositions 1, 2, 4, 7, 11, 13, 14, 15, 16, 17, 26, 19, 23, 24, 30, 32, 34, 35, 36, 40

THE THREE WAYS OF KNOWING

Part II: Propositions 40, 41, 43, 44, 45, 46, 47, 48, 49

WILL AND VIRTUE

Part II: Proposition 49